BUILDING SELF-

P562

SELF-DEVELOPMENT

BUILDING SELF-ESTEEM

How to replace self-doubt with
confidence and well-being

William Stewart

YOU'RE SHY,
AREN'T YOU?

How To Books

Cartoons by Mike Flanagan

British Library Cataloguing in Publication Data

A catalogue record for this book is available from the British Library.

© Copyright 1998 William Stewart.

Published by How To Books Ltd, 3 Newtec Place,
Magdalen Road, Oxford OX4 1RE, United Kingdom.
Tel: (01865) 793806. Fax: (01865) 248780.
email: info@howtobooks.co.uk
www.howtobooks.co.uk

First edition 1998
Second impression 1999

Note: The material contained in this book is set out in good faith for general
guidance and no liability can be accepted for loss or expense incurred as a
result of relying in particular circumstances on statements made in this book.
The law and regulations may be complex and liable to change, and readers
should check the current position with the relevant authorities before making
personal arrangements.

Cover design by Shireen Nathoo Design
Cover image PhotoDisc

Produced for How To Books by Deer Park Productions.
Typeset by Concept Communications (Design & Print) Ltd, Crayford, Kent.
Printed and bound by Cromwell Press, Trowbridge, Wiltshire.

Contents

List of Illustrations

IS THIS YOU?

Low self-esteem   Low self-confidence

Easily put down by people

Getting married   Finding work stressful

Facing redundancy

Coping with bereavement   Can't cope any more

Prone to irrational thinking

Lacking direction in life   Suffering from discrimination

Feeling anxious

Facing major life changes   Struggling with ill-health

Overwhelmed with worry

Often down in the dumps   Lacking belief in yourself

Overwhelmed by shyness

Plagued by negative thoughts   Can't control your emotions

Ruled by pessimism

Not a good communicator   Struggling with conflicts

Finding change difficult

Drained of energy   Wanting more openness

Seeking more independence

Have difficulty showing affection   Ruled by work

Have difficulty being assertive

Preface

My interest in self-esteem has developed over the years as a counsellor, as I observed that almost all people who come for counselling are, at the time, suffering from a lowered self-esteem. I have identified three groups of people with different types of self-esteem problems.

Firstly there are those who are normally confident and self-assertive, and would have rated their self-esteem as high, but show indications of their self-esteem having taken a knock. This led me to propose that self-esteem is not a fixed quality of personality. It is not like the colour of one's eyes, or one's height. Rather, it is more fragile, like our body which can be attacked by a multitude of invaders to make us feel sick and below par.

Events come along which attack even the strongest person and lower their self-esteem. For such people, once the event or circumstance has been dealt with, self-esteem returns to its previous level, or even higher; for having successfully dealt with a crisis of confidence, they feel the stronger.

The second group are those who have a consistently low self-esteem, who never think of themselves as having any worth. These are people whose self-esteem has never been fostered; who from the moment they were born received more negative inputs than positive; who feel that they are nothing more than an encumbrance. Chronically low self-esteem acts like a dark filter on a camera; life never seems to have any joy or brilliance.

A third group are those who find refuge in their role or work. There they enjoy a feeling of being needed; they are respected for their contribution to society; they are worth something. But the moment they leave work, they feel worthless again. Their self-esteem is compartmentalised; without work they almost cease to exist. People with work-related self-esteem are particularly vulnerable, for when work comes to an end they have nothing left. When the gates close – metaphorically – their self-esteem vanishes.

This book brings together many different issues, but all with the central purpose of helping you understand that transient thing called self-esteem. A second aim is to help you assess your own level of self-esteem. The third aim is to present ways in which you can help yourself build your self-esteem, and replace self-doubt with confidence and well-being. If in the process you find yourself able to help someone else to do this, then so much the better; for often as we help others so we ourselves find strength. May your journey prove to be worthwhile.

William Stewart

1
Defining Self-Esteem

INTRODUCTION

If everybody had a realistic and healthy view of themselves this book need not be written. But the fact is, many of us evaluate ourselves negatively. This chapter looks at what self-esteem is and how the foundations of low self-esteem are laid at a young age. This being so, what can be done? Can the ravages of faulty beliefs about self be reversed? One of the premises of this book is that what has been learned can be unlearned, even though the process is a painful struggle. Low self-esteem, while its roots can often be traced to childhood or adolescence, can happen at any stage of life.

High self-esteem contributes to an overall sense of psychological well-being, mainly because high self-esteem seems to be linked to feelings of optimism, and of being able to exert some control over events. High self-esteem is also linked to being able to face difficulties and setbacks in life, whereas low self-esteem seems to be linked to pessimism and lowered expectations.

DEFINING SELF-ESTEEM

Self-esteem is the value we place on ourselves. A high self-esteem is a positive value; a low self-esteem results from attaching negative values to ourselves or some part of ourselves. Some of the questions asked about self-esteem are:

- Where does evaluation of self come from?
- How does self-esteem differ from person to person?
- How is self-esteem enhanced, maintained or protected?
- How is self-esteem measured?

Ten principal ways by which we evaluate ourselves positively

1. We have a firm belief in our attributes, accomplishments and abilities.

2. We face ourselves honestly but realistically.

3. We are willing to listen to other people, but not to be swayed by every different opinion.

4. We accept other people's views, but also recognise that they might be wrong.

5. We use others as models, but are not put down if our achievement doesn't match theirs.

6. We are able to learn from self-perception and self-evaluation, and change, but are not a psychological chameleon.

7. We are aware of the effects of our behaviour on other people; we have a public conscience.

8. We are able to take a positive view of self and life.

9. We are able to set clear goals and work steadily towards them.

10. We are not overwhelmed by our faults and failings, but do something to overcome them.

Ten principal ways by which we evaluate ourselves negatively

1. We compare ourselves unfavourably with other people.

2. We denigrate ourselves in a global way, rather than saying, 'I am not good at (for example) DIY, but I am good at (for example) playing the piano.'

3. We say to ourselves and others, 'I'm not worth very much, but you are.'

4. We believe that other people have a right to exist, but not us.

5. We believe what other people say about us.

6. We rely too much on the approval of other people, such as our peers.

7. We rely on being popular, which may be at the expense of self-worth.

8. We believe that our success is due to luck, while other people's success is due to ability.

9. We believe that being servile, submissive and passive are correct ways of behaving.

10. We believe that other people, particularly those in authority, are always right.

DECIDING TO BE YOURSELF

Don't believe that everything famous people say or have said must be correct. Sigmund Freud, and other psychologists, as well as prominent people in other spheres, such as theology, supported the idea that women are 'failed' or 'defective' men; creatures of lesser ability, and less creative. Freud further believed that when a woman was competent and self-assured, or intelligent, that she was striving to be a man, suffering from what he called a 'masculine complex'. Carl Jung did not go as far as Freud, but he saw men as the creators and women as their assistants.

The Bible puts forward the view that man (Adam) is the head, and woman (Eve) is his helper. The whole of the Bible is male dominated, and much of fundamental Christian doctrine and practice still keeps women in a submissive relationship to men. This raises the question, how far does such a difference in the treatment of the sexes influence self-esteem?

Gender will be discussed further in Chapter 6, but for now it is important to recognise that deep within the individual psyche are years of indoctrination – both explicit and implicit – that there is a fundamental difference between men and women: men are superior, and women inferior. This puts both men and women in a difficult position.

If males are indoctrinated to believe that females are inferior, then they will deny themselves all the so-called 'feminine qualities' – tenderness, intuitiveness and caring. Likewise, if females are brought up to believe that men are superior, then they will deny themselves the so-called 'masculine qualities' – intelligence, thinking and strength.

Yet many men are more tender and compassionate than some women, and many women are more ruthless and aggressive than some men. If men and women do not acknowledge their essential characteristics, for fear of what other people might think, they are only working on half-charged batteries. The result is a lowered self-esteem, because they are not being themselves.

I'M THE GREATEST

Some people have an inflated self-esteem, and this can be just as damaging as a low-self-esteem. Such people are often referred to as 'big heads'. They are the ones who attempt to bolster their self-esteem at the expense of others' self-esteem. It is as if they can only feel good about themselves, by standing on the heads of other people and thus putting them down. In psychiatry, the term 'narcissism' denotes an excessive degree of self-esteem or self-involvement, a condition that is usually a form of emotional immaturity.

Self-esteem is not a fixed quality or attribute; it is affected by such factors as stress, poor health, bereavement, loss of job and retirement. Most people cope with these events, but people whose self-esteem is fragile can be thrown into emotional confusion.

Characteristics of people with a high self-esteem

1. They generally have positive (and realistic) expectations of their efforts and their outcomes.

2. They are generally not anxious about life, and take more risks.

3. They are likely to find evidence to credit themselves for their successes.

4. They are likely to accept responsibility for their failures.

5. They generally feel themselves equal to other people.

6. They are likely to engage in self-improvement activities.

7. They are relatively happy, satisfied with their lives and reasonably well-adjusted.

8. They generally experience positive emotions.

Characteristics of people with a lowered self-esteem

1. They often find it difficult to see anything positive about what they do.

2. They tend to be more anxious about life, and prefer feeling safe to taking risks.

3. They tend not to take credit for their successes.

4. They are over-concerned with taking responsibility for their failures, and looking for evidence that they have done poorly.

5. They feel inferior to other people.

6. They tend not to be motivated by self-improvement, but do all they can to protect themselves against failure or disappointment.

7. They are not very happy, not satisfied with their lives, and not well-adjusted.

8. They are prone to experience depression, hopelessness and suicidal thoughts.

Caution:

It must be pointed out that the above characteristics are generalisations, and while they apply to many people, there are exceptions in both high and low self-esteem. In fact, as with all discussion of personality, self-esteem should not be regarded as an 'either/or', but rather as a scale from High to Low, with many gradations between the two extremes. A related point is that people can be 'high' in some aspects of self-esteem and low in others. The challenge is to work on those areas we know to be low, and that influence our life in a negative sense, and try to move them up a notch or two on the scale.

EXPLORING THE ROOTS

Bonding

Bonding is the formation of a close personal relationship (as between a mother and child) especially through frequent or constant association. The process of bonding between mother and baby starts long before the birth. If the baby in the womb responds to noise, then how much more is it likely to respond to feelings of already being loved, or the reverse, of not being wanted, or of fear on the mother's part that she will not be a good mother?

For nine months, the environment within the womb is all-important to the developing baby; the mother's emotional and physical state plays a vital role in creating this environment. Sometimes events take over and the baby is catapulted prematurely into the world. Difficulty of delivery and premature birth add to the problems of the mother bonding with the new baby. Bonding is not just at birth; it is for life.

Babies born prematurely may induce feelings of great fear in the mother; when born with defects, the mother might not be able to accept the baby. Bonding is then fraught with difficulty. Early bonding difficulties are likely to lead to a decrease in the new mother's self-esteem. When this happens, the feelings are likely to be transmitted to the child.

Paternal bonding is said to be as important as maternal bonding, and certainly for the development of high self-esteem, the role of the father is necessary. The developing child needs to experience the feelings of being wanted and loved by both parents. When this love is deficient, the growing child is in danger of developing a low self-esteem.

Summary of bonding

● Bonding between mother and baby starts at conception.

● A mother's physical and emotional state influences the environment in the womb.

- Bonding is influenced by premature birth, defects in the baby, separation due to illness, or conditions such as depression.

- Paternal bonding is important.

Attachment

Attachment is the emotional bond between infants and their caregivers. The quality of that attachment is crucial in the development of the self-concept and a feeling of self-worth.

Attachment theory was developed by the English psychologist John Bowlby in the late 1960s. He argued that this early relationship is the foundation for all later relationships. Early attachment influences adult behaviour, particularly during illness, distress or when afraid. Separation anxiety and homesickness are thought to be a result of faulty attachment. The understanding of grief, bereavement, mourning, loss and loneliness have all been enhanced by attachment theory.

Secure attachment enhances feelings of self-worth, as the developing infant experiences feelings of being valued. **Insecure attachment** is experienced by infants when the caregiver is anxious and avoids making emotional contact with the infant, or is ambivalent about the relationship. In the first instance, the child is likely to avoid making emotional contact with other people; in the second, the child is likely to be preoccupied with relationships, clinging to caregivers, but also easily angered by them.

Attachment to some other caregiver is thus an important factor in the development of a healthy self-esteem.

Summary of attachment

- Attachment between infant and caregiver is essential for healthy development.

- Attachment can be disrupted by events that separate mother from infant.

- Behavioural difficulties in childhood may result from inadequate attachment.

- Secure attachment is one influence in the development of self-esteem.

- Insecure attachment can lead to relationship difficulties in adult life.

Approval

Approval is a crucial element in the development of a child's self-worth and self-esteem. One definition of approval is 'to pronounce to be good, to commend'. Two other words linked with approval are acceptance and affirmation.

Approval, by parents or other significant figures in the life of the child (including siblings, particularly older ones, who exercise a profound influence on younger ones), is a form of control. People who as children have experienced little or no approval, in adult life often seem to go to extraordinary lengths to gain approval, almost as if the deficit can never be made up.

Approval is:

● Recognition which confirms our unique identity, and does not try to make us be someone we are not.

● Acceptance of what we have to offer, without any preconceived ideas of what we should be or ought to be.

The results of approval are:

● Feelings of security.

● Not being rejected because our abilities, opinions and what we think, feel or do, do not match up with other people's expectations of us.

● Affirmation of our uniqueness and our existence.

● Increased status and a sense of recognition.

● A bond established between approver and approved.

● Permission to take control of our lives, and responsibility for our actions.

The opposite of approval is rejection, and one of the principal ways we use rejection is by always passing judgement, always putting the other person in the wrong. Children are particularly prone to all that goes with judgement, and when this is reinforced with conditional love – 'I will love you if . . .' – then the child has little solid ground on which to build a healthy self-esteem. The poem in Figure 1, from an unknown source, encapsulates the discussion on approval.

School experiences

Not all rejection comes from within the home. A child might live within a loving and caring family but be exposed to harsh criticism,

If children live with criticism, they learn to condemn.

If children live with hostility, they learn to fight.

If children live with ridicule, they learn to be shy.

If children live with shame, they learn to be guilty.

If children live with tolerance, they learn to be patient.

If children live with encouragement, they learn confidence.

If children live with praise, they learn to appreciate.

If children live with fairness, they learn justice.

If children live with security, they learn faith.

If children live with approval, they learn to like themselves.

If children live with acceptance, they learn to find love in the world.

Fig. 1. Influences on children.

rejection, ridicule and abuse at school, from both teachers and other pupils. Such negative nicknames as 'fatty', 'big ears', 'four eyes', 'skinny' and so on may chip away at an undeveloped self-esteem. Even nicknames such as 'honey', 'angel', 'pet' and 'poppet', thought to be complimentary, may reduce the child to something less than human.

Acceptance by one's peers is an important factor in the life of any child. There are a multitude of reasons why a child's self-esteem may be undermined rather than enhanced. For many, schooldays are purgatory, and learning is often affected as a consequence, further chipping away at self-esteem. Most children learn to cope, and will, provided other relationships are there to redress the harm done at school and by peers. Peer pressure is so often tied in with gaining approval; and the young person whose self-esteem is already damaged by nqn-approval may not be able to resist peer demands on behaviour.

Growing up
Growing up means coping with dramatic bodily and emotional changes; it also means the prospect of taking on adult responsibilities. Young people

start to form their own relationships, and some of those may not enhance self-esteem. Sexual experiences may severely damage a person's self-esteem – at any age. Most people want and need intimacy, but taking on the responsibilities of an intimate relationship, if it does not work out, can be very damaging.

Self-esteem does not stop developing at the legal age of maturity; it goes on being enhanced or damaged throughout life, but the roots of a healthy self-esteem are laid down in childhood. Life events often seem to conspire against us, and knocks, when they come, can easily cause our self-esteem to plummet; for example, following a messy divorce, the death of one's spouse or partner, the birth of a baby with a disability, or the onset of illness. Nobody can stick a patch on our self-esteem; all we can do is pick ourselves up and start to rebuild a stronger self-esteem. By understanding ourselves more, we can start the uphill climb towards positive self-esteem.

CASE STUDY

Jenny: I couldn't do that!

Jenny, mother of two sons, was left a well-provided-for widow in her mid-forties. Her friend Helen suggested that Jenny apply for a job in the children's ward of the local hospital. Jenny had trained as a nanny, but said she lacked confidence to do 'real nursing', and was unconvinced of her ability.

Her two teenage sons told her to stop putting herself down, to believe in herself and not to keep saying that all she was good for was bringing them up. Jenny admitted that she did put herself down, and she needed every encouragement to tackle anything new. It had taken all her husband's power of persuasion to get Jenny to learn to drive, but she passed first time. Jenny had done a lot to overcome her feelings of diffidence and self-doubt since marrying Bill at the age of twenty.

She knew very well that her dominant mother had pushed her down to the extent that she found it difficult to make any decisions. 'You can't do that.' 'You're no good.' 'You can't cook.' 'You'll never manage a family if you're left a widow.' 'You, a nurse? Don't make me laugh. You'd be sick. The only thing you'd be good for is emptying bedpans.' When Jenny did get her well-paid job as a nanny, her mother was again dismissive. 'It won't last.' Whenever Jenny felt uncertain, her mother's carping voice echoed in her mind, and often in her dreams; then she would wake up crying.

Three days a week Jenny donned her nursing auxiliary uniform, and she was soon a valued member of the small team. It was with the children and their parents that she came into her own. Jenny had a natural gift for being a child herself, and the children responded. No child could remain fractious for very long; for most of the time Jenny found just the right thing to do or say. Parents anxious about a forthcoming operation found quiet confidence in Jenny's words, or comfort over a cup of tea as she talked with them after they had received dreaded news, or as they watched their lovely child slip slowly away. Jenny was not technical, just human.

Comment

Jenny's battle to improve her self-esteem was a long and painful one, helped by her marriage to an understanding and supportive husband. But therein lay a trap. The more she became involved in being 'the wife', the less she found it necessary to stretch herself, and settled into a comfortable rut of domesticity. The early chipping away at her self-esteem by her dominant mother, who rarely showed approval, took a great deal of repairing. Children who grow up in an environment full of put-downs and criticism often become adults with a less than adequate self-esteem. Jenny's mother instilled in her the belief that she would never succeed. The fact that Jenny did succeed, far more than she gave herself credit for, was, for her, a major milestone.

Exercise: The ideal self versus the actual self

We all possess an *actual* and an *ideal* self. The ideal self is what we know we could be, should be or would like to be. The ideal self is influenced by:

● parental expectations

● instructions received on how to behave

● the values of parents

● the values of heroic figures from real life, biography and fiction.

Low self-esteem operates in the gap between the actual self and the ideal self.

From the following list of qualities and values, make two lists: one to represent your *ideal* self and another your *actual* self. Be honest with yourself.

When you have worked out your two lists, spend time deciding how far the discrepancy between the ideal self and the actual self influences your self-esteem, and why. This analysis might take a great deal of time. When you have done this, decide which quality or value you feel you could work on to move it, even a little way, from the actual to the ideal. You might find it helpful to ask someone who knows you very well to comment on how accurately you know yourself.

Adventurous	Hesitant	Pessimistic
Affectionate	Imaginative	Practical
Agreeable	Immature	Quiet
Aloof	Impatient	Relaxed
Ambitious	Impulsive	Reliable
Arrogant	Inattentive	Rigid
Assertive	Incompetent	Sad
Attentive	Industrious	Secretive
Boring	Insecure	Secure
Cautious	Intellectual	Self-confident
Cold	Interesting	Sensitive
Compassionate	Introverted	Serious
Competent	Lazy	Severe
Contradictory	Light-hearted	Shy
Conventional	Likeable	Sociable
Demanding	Lively	Stable
Dominant	Mature	Submissive
Dull	Mean	Tense
Easy-going	Modern	Tolerant
Exacting	Modest	Unaspiring
Extroverted	Moody	Unattractive
Flexible	Open	Unreliable
Friendly	Optimistic	Unresolved
Generous	Passive	Unsure
Happy	Patient	
Hard	Persistent	

SUMMARY

1. Self-esteem has its roots in early life.

2. Self-esteem is not a fixed quantity, it can be enhanced or eroded by life events, and varies from culture to culture.

3. Positive self-esteem seems to be linked to feelings of optimism, whereas negative self-esteem is linked to feelings of pessimism.

4. Teaching by some psychologists and churches reinforces the stereotypes of male dominance and female submission.

5. Inflated self-esteem may be symptomatic of narcissism.

6. Bonding and attachment of infant to mother (or other caregiver) are essential to the development of a positive self-esteem.

7. People deprived of approval and acceptance from parents and other significant figures may spend the remainder of their lives frantically seeking what they missed as children.

8. Abuse, bullying and name-calling at school is a powerful influence on the development of negative self-worth.

9. Uncertainty about body-image at adolescence is a powerful weapon in developing low self-esteem.

10. Lack of achievement at school, in college and at work is likely to reinforce negative self-esteem.

11. Traumatic life events may also contribute to a lowering of self-esteem.

12. By developing self-awareness, we can start to build a positive self-esteem.

2
Understanding Health Issues

INTRODUCTION

Health is more than the absence of disease; it is a state of well-being influenced by the interaction of our body, mind, emotions and behaviour. St Paul said, 'If one organ suffers, they all suffer together. If one flourishes, they all rejoice together' (*The New English Bible*, 1Cor. 12: 26). Paul was using the body as an analogy of the Church, but what he said applies to actual bodies – health and well-being means caring for every part. When we abuse or neglect one part, all other parts suffer, the body will feel 'out of sorts' and will misfunction. Perfect functioning of the body depends upon all parts working together in balance and harmony.

ASSESSING YOUR WELL-BEING

Physical well-being

How many of these are a problem to you:

- Difficulty getting to sleep or staying asleep?

- Headaches and pains in the head?

- Indigestion or sickness?

- Feeling unaccountably tired/exhausted?

- Needing tranquillisers to get through the day?

- Decrease in sexual interest?

- Shortness of breath or feeling dizzy?

- Feeling that your heart is pounding out of your chest?

- Difficulty sleeping without taking pills?

- Feeling worn out at the end of the day?

Mental well-being

How many of these are a problem to you:

- Being irritable and easily losing your temper?

- Worrying about mistakes, actions or decisions you've made?

- Being suspicious of other people?

- Not being able to cope with interruptions, e.g. the phone?

- Not wanting to face another day?

- Lying awake worrying about problems?

- Thinking that people are out to get you?

- Thinking that life has nothing worthwhile to offer you?

- Feeling sad and tearful?

- Feeling that life is passing you by?

Emotional well-being

How many of these are a problem to you:

- Feeling bored with everything?

- Feeling you are not valued?

- Having bouts of moodiness?

- Snappy with people?

- Disturbed by feeling out of control of yourself?

- Feeling you want to cry for no reason?

- Always needing to seek approval?

- Often being angry?

- Feeling you're going to explode?

- Feeling tense and anxious?

Behavioural well-being

How many of these are a problem to you:

- Dreading going out and meeting people?
- Feeling that people treat you unfairly?
- Feeling isolated and alone?
- Resentful of what other people have achieved in life?
- Feeling trapped in your situation?
- Not wishing to get up and go to work?
- Looking for opportunities to spend time away from the job?
- Frequently late for work?
- Failing to meet targets?
- Reporting sick when you're not really ill?

UNDERSTANDING SPIRITUALITY

Spirituality is about more than 'being religious'. It may include religion and worship, but it goes beyond them. Spirituality is a quality or condition of being spiritual; attachment to or regard for things of the spirit as opposed to material or worldly interests. Spirituality also means the finer perceptions of life. Spirituality is not limited to creeds or beliefs.

Roberto Assagioli, founder of Psychosynthesis, an integrated approach to psychiatry, writes that spiritual psychosynthesis is a gradual awakening, a journey towards integration and spiritual realisation. But this journey of spiritual development is a long and arduous adventure through strange lands full of surprises, difficulties and sometimes dangers. Trying to build self-esteem without also developing spirituality would be like building a house without windows.

Assessing your spiritual well-being

Over the period of the past year:

- How frequently have you given time for your personal development?
- What inspirational books or tapes have you read or listened to?
- What have you achieved, enjoyed doing, done especially well?
- What have you contributed to the wider improvement of society?

- What have you done to improve the quality of someone's life?

- How have you developed your personal qualities?

- What have you done to develop your self-awareness?

- What spiritual development have you engaged in?

- What gifts have you shared with others?

- What have you done to take on new ideas of living?

Exercise: Developing your spirituality

Words are symbols which evoke ideas and images that affect our feelings and thoughts.

1. Find a quiet place where you will not be disturbed.

2. Get into a relaxed state.

3. Choose a word from the list below. Close your eyes and mentally repeat the word. Then, still concentrating on that one word, observe any ideas and images which your mind associates with it.

4. Reflect on the meaning of the word, then record the results.

5. If you prefer, print the words on plain white cards, using the associated colours indicated.

Calm	(dark green)	Joy	(yellow)
Comprehension	(yellow)	Love	(blue)
Confidence	(reddish orange)	Patience	(green)
Courage	(red)	Peace	(white on black)
Energy	(brick red)	Serenity	(deep blue)
Enthusiasm	(brick red)	Silence	(blue)
Goodness	(gold)	Simplicity	(gold)
Gratitude	(gold)	Will	(red)
Harmony	(green)	Wisdom	(dark blue)

Some of the listed words may cause negative reactions in us because we feel as if the words are accusing us, making us painfully aware of our lack of these qualities, and this irritates us. If this happens to you, do not despair. Continue to concentrate on that particular word and associated feelings.

A variation is to imagine you are looking at a number of doors, each with the particular word on it. Decide to go through one of those doors and explore what lies behind it. You may feel able to travel only a little way – never mind: two steps along a previously not travelled way are two more steps towards greater self-understanding. Some other time you may want to continue that particular journey. You may also discover that some doors are easier to open than others. Never force an unwilling door. Mark it, and return to it some other time.

End of session exercise

Every time you engage in exercises involving imagery, it is advisable to finish off with the following routine:

1. Rapidly sketch over the session in your mind.

2. Make a few notes of what took place and any insights you have received.

3. Go round and touch various objects to 'ground' you.

4. Stand upright, stretch your hands above your head, and as you slowly lower them to your sides, repeat, several times, 'I am . . . Today's date is . . . and I am here (name of the room and place).'

LEARNING TO MANAGE HEALTH DIFFICULTIES

Illness of any kind can sap your self-esteem. Self-esteem is pushed to low depths in such conditions as eating disorders, disabilities, traumas involving mind or body. When you are constantly tired, often in pain, feeling restricted and trapped within an ailing body because of some incurable disease, when energy plummets and you feel constantly down or anxious, self-esteem takes a battering.

Health problems create a discrepancy between the ideal self and the actual self, and this discrepancy often brings guilt with it.

This chapter will deal with anxiety and depression as two of the main difficulties, one or both of which may be present in many illnesses and conditions of ill-health. (Anxiety will be discussed further in Chapter 7.)

EXPERIENCING ANXIETY

Anxiety is a physical and emotional response to anticipated situations – real or imagined – when no appropriate action is finally taken. Mild anxiety is a common feeling, experienced by most people at some time in life. It is a feeling of uneasiness or apprehension, often accompanied by one or more of the following **indicators**:

- sweat on the upper lip and forehead

- sweaty palms

- dry mouth
- dilated pupils
- increased heart rate and breathing
- stomach feels 'knotted', there may also be diarrhoea and/or vomiting
- desire to pass water frequently
- limbs feel like jelly.

Exercise: Identifying anxious events

Most times, normal anxiety is based on anticipating some actual event: attending an interview for a new job, having to tackle a difficult assignment, taking an examination, giving a speech, being admitted to hospital, visiting the dentist, taking a driving test.

1. What incidents in your life do you associate with feeling any of the indicators listed above? These may be places you have visited; people you have met; events; situations in which you were involved.

2. Do you feel more anxious about actual or anticipated events?

3. Can you remember the first time you experienced these feelings?

4. Did you feel like this when you:
   - started school?
   - were punished for something?
   - started your first job?
   - were waiting at the wedding altar?
   - went to a funeral of a friend/relative?
   - took your first aeroplane trip?
   - were admitted to hospital?

Not all events that produce feelings of anxiety are necessarily unpleasant. Getting married or being presented with an award are two events that could be termed 'pleasant'; yet they often produce feelings of anxiety. Generally, however, the anxiety associated with such events is not long-lasting. When the event has passed, feelings generally return quite quickly to normal, in much the same way as the heart rate, in a healthy individual, returns to normal after exercise.

Normal anxiety, in small amounts, is biologically necessary for survival. Anxiety in doses too large for us to handle leads to panic, and panic produces irrational behaviour. When anxiety is chronic and not traceable to any specific cause, or when it interferes with normal activity, the sufferer is in need of expert help.

ASSESSING DEPRESSION

Illness and disability alter one's self-esteem and may plunge a person possessed of a low-esteem into a state of depression. Depression leads to feelings of isolation and difference often setting the sufferer apart from other people, who resort to such patronising advice as, 'Pull yourself together', 'Look on the bright side', 'Think positively', 'It can't be as black as all that.'

Eight indicators of depression

1. Loss of enjoyment in life.

2. Sadness.

3. Guilt and worthlessness.

4. Suspiciousness.

5. Loss of energy and interest.

6. Disturbance of:

    ● sleep

    ● appetite and weight

    ● time sense

    ● sexual function.

7. Ideas of suicide.

8. Retardation (slowing up of all functions) and agitation.

At this stage it is worth making the comment that the word 'depression' is often used carelessly to mean anything from feeling blue, down in the dumps, low, to being fed up, dejected or discouraged. Such misuse of the word demeans the true meaning of depression.

Assessing high and low self-esteem and depression

● High self-esteem equates to feelings of integration, freedom, positive emotion and availability of energy, and well-being.

● Lowered self-esteem is likely to be accompanied by unhappiness, anger, sense of threat, fatigue, withdrawal, tension, disorganisation, feelings of constraint, conflict and inhibition.

- Very low self-esteem often results in a feeling of worthlessness.

- People with high self-esteem feel an inward sense of approval.

- People with low self-esteem feel an inward sense of disapproval.

- Esteem for others is as necessary as esteem for oneself.

- People who have little self-esteem, or esteem for others, are already programmed for feeling helpless or hopeless in the face of loss.

- People with a high self-esteem accept loss more readily than people with low self-esteem in whom loss often leads to hopelessness.

- Loss of self-esteem may result from the symbolic losses of, for example, power, status, roles, and values, all of which influence, to one degree or another, the way we live our life.

- Self-esteem is at the very core of our personality, and low self-esteem is characteristic of a disturbed sense of well-being.

KEEPING YOUR SELF-ESTEEM BUCKET FILLED

Virginia Satir in her book, *People Making*, introduces the idea of the 'self-esteem bucket'. The idea is that we come into life with a perfect bucket, and throughout life, starting from the moment we are born, the bucket starts to fill up with all the good things that together make up our healthy self-esteem. All negative inputs act like holes being pierced in the bucket. If the inputs never catch up with the leakages, the end result is low self-esteem.

Using autosuggestion

One way to help keep the bucket topped up is to use autosuggestion, a self-help method developed by Emile Coué in the 1920s, using twice-daily repetition of the mantra, 'Every day, and in every way, I am becoming better and better.' When using autosuggestion, concentrate on the positive. Don't say, ' I am becoming less (for example, anxious)', but rather, 'I am becoming more relaxed.' Relaxed is the desired state. Couple this with positive imagination, creating situations in your mind where you are confident.

Assessing your self-esteem bucket

- Who was significant in your childhood?

- Who loved you unconditionally?

- Who never showed you love?

- Who praised you and your achievements?

- Who accepted you?

- Who rejected you?

- Who showed you affection?

- Who brushed off your affection?

- Who most criticised you?

Complete the following statements for yourself:

- I was most criticised for . . .

- The positive labels I carry around with me from the past are . . .

- The negative labels I carry around with me from the past are . . .

- The effects people from the past still have on my self-esteem are . .

Exercise: Repairing the leakages in your bucket

Don't wait around for someone, or some event, to block the holes. Start doing it yourself! List the things you feel you want to change. Arrange them in order from the 'easiest' to the 'hardest'. Make up your mind that just as your self-esteem was attacked by your believing what other people said about you, or did to you, so you have the power to reverse the damage.

Imagine a bucket clearly labelled, 'My self-esteem bucket'. You may find it helpful to imagine your name on it.

Use autosuggestion. Start with one hole, the one thing you feel would be the easiest to block, then create a positive image instead of the negative one that started the leakage. If you identified the leakage as your grandmother always calling you 'stupid', recreate the scene to one in which she is telling you how clever you are. Hear her say, 'You can do anything you wish if you put your mind to it.' When you feel comfortable that you have reduced the leakage of one hole, move on to the next. You may discover that as you work on one, you need to return to a hole you worked on earlier. Persevere, and they may all gradually get smaller.

LEARNING TO LISTEN TO YOUR BODY

Body awareness is often the first step towards increasing well-being. Many of us listen more to the weather forecast than we listen to our bodies. Certain therapeutic body techniques are based on the principle that character is intimately related to posture, structure, energy flow and tensions. Therapy is directed towards releasing blocked tension by applying pressure, by palpating or by massaging.

Walking tall

F.M. Alexander, who developed the Alexander technique, taught that the spinal energy should flow upwards so that all movement comes from the head. An imaginary hook pulls the spine up into the correct alignment, that of a gently curved vertical. When we are feeling low, we tend to slouch, as if carrying the world on our shoulders. Thus feelings influence behaviour in the way we walk. The very act of straightening up – walking tall – straightens the back. You can't carry your burden on a straight back. Walking tall induces a feeling of well-being and confidence. Chronic muscular tension interferes with free functioning of the whole person.

Learning to be aware of your body

If you are serious about learning a new skill, you will spend a great deal of time, patience and energy doing all you can to become proficient. An accomplished pianist does not achieve that competence without a great deal of effort and concentration. The same applies to any achievement. Learning to build your self-esteem requires every bit as much effort and dedication. It also means a change in attitude and thinking. You may not acquire these new skills immediately, but if you believe in them, and practise them *daily*, several times daily if possible, you will succeed, and they will start to work for you.

Exercise: Learning external and internal awareness

External awareness

This exercise can be done anywhere, preferably somewhere not too noisy. Focus your attention on what is happening around you. Say to yourself (aloud if you can), 'I am aware of . . .' (here use all your five senses – what can you see, hear, smell, feel, even taste?).

Internal awareness

When you have done the above, focus on what is happening within your body (e.g. 'My hands are feeling cold; I feel hungry; my eyes are watering; my heart is beating strongly; I feel sleepy').

Switch back and forth between external and internal awareness. Use this exercise when you have any free moments throughout the day, to become really aware of the difference between your inner and outer worlds.

Exercise: Learning to survey your body

1. Lie down, or sit in a comfortable chair, with your eyes closed.

2. Focus on every part of your body in turn.

3. Identify any part where you feel tense and cannot relax, and mentally tell it to relax. All muscular tension is self-produced, so you have the power to alter it.

4. At this point, be aware of any life situation that may be causing the tension in your body and what you could do to change it.

5. Lie on your bed and imagine a pulley attached to your head, through your spinal column, pulling you dead straight. Assess how aligned your body is. Shift a merest fraction at a time until you feel more aligned.

6. Stand against a wall, with as many parts of your back – calves, buttocks, shoulders, back of head – touching the wall, making sure that you reduce the hollow in your back to the absolute minimum.

IMPROVING YOUR SELF-ESTEEM

Four questionnaires, the first in Figure 2 below and the others in Chapters 3, 4 and 5, measure the Body, Mind, Emotions and Behaviour parts of self-esteem.

HOW I FEEL ABOUT MY BODY – PART 1

From List A, select ten parts of the body you consider to be the most important to you. Then arrange these ten parts in order of priority from **least value** to **most value**.

List A

Appearance, arms, belly, breasts, buttocks, chest/bust, ears, eyes, face, feet, fingers, forehead, hair, hands, height, hips, internal organs, legs, mouth, neck, nose, sexual organs, shoulders, size, skin, teeth, tongue, voice, weight.

Assessment of Part 1

1 ....   *The part of my body I value least*

2 ....

3 ....

4 ....

5 ....

6 ....

Fig. 2. Assessing your body and self-esteem..

7 ....

8 ....

9 ....

10 ....   *The part of my body I value most*

HOW I FEEL ABOUT MY BODY – PART 2

For each of the ten parts of your body, choose from List B a word or words to describe that part. You may add any words which are not there.

List B

Aggressive, beautiful, bandy, chubby, clean, cold, corpulent, cruel, damaged, delicate, desirable, destructive, detestable, dirty, feminine, gentle, handsome, harmless, healthy, kind, lean, lovely, masculine, misshapen, obese, open, passive, pleasant, plump, podgy, rejecting, sick, skinny, slim, stocky, strong, thin, tough, ugly, understanding, unpleasant, valuable, warm, weak, well-shaped, whole, worthless.

Assessment of Part 2

The word or words I would use to describe each part:

1 ....

2 ....

3 ....

4 ....

5 ....

6 ....

7 ....

8 ....

9 ....

10 ....

- Now make a list of the reasons why you chose those words to describe the parts of your body.

- How does your regard or disregard for your body influence your overall self-esteem?

Fig. 2. (Continued.)

In each of the four questionnaires assess how **Dissatisfied/Satisfied** you are.

CASE STUDY

Jim's self-esteem bucket

Jim had been a fairly confident man until a relationship he had invested in collapsed around his ears, leaving him hurt and angry, and feeling worthless. As he explored his feelings with his counsellor, he realised that he was recreating several scenes from his adolescence. He had never felt secure about mixing with girls, so he found refuge in 'manly' sports and activities. He tracked some of his feelings of insecurity with girls to his father's put-downs. 'You'll never be manly enough to get a woman, all you're interested in is your cissy art and music.' This was one of the holes Jim worked to repair. In his imagination he recreated his father saying positive things about him. Then he made a patch and stuck it on the hole. Even though the hole still leaked a bit, he felt he had the tools with which to work on substituting positive for negative beliefs.

SUMMARY

1. Good health is a vital component in the development of a positive self-esteem.

2. Illness, disability, events and circumstances influence low self-esteem.

3. Self-esteem is influenced by physical, mental, emotional, behavioural and spiritual aspects.

4. Anxiety and depression are two major states often present in other illnesses.

5. Events in life often induce anxiety, and sensitise a person to feeling anxious.

6. Depression erodes self-esteem because it isolates the sufferer.

7. The self-esteem bucket starts to be filled from early childhood.

8. Holes in the self-esteem bucket are made by everything that is negative.

9. Body awareness is often the first step towards increasing well-being.

10. Remember, your body is the only one you will ever have; care for it.

11. Own your body in every aspect as a precious asset.

12. Nobody can improve your self-esteem for you.

3
Mastering Effective Communication

DEFINING COMMUNICATION

Communication occurs when what takes place in one person's mind influences another person's mind, so that both people are reasonably satisfied that they have reached understanding. Communication is not just about words; communication conveys feelings and demonstrates behaviour. Unless we can convey the message, our communication will have failed. Being able to 'feel' or imagine what it is like to be the other person, something called empathy, ensures our communication will be effective.

Communication is a channel of influence, the cement which binds a relationship together. When we communicate with each other we listen to the words and at the same time we try to 'hear between the lines'. Communication is sharing of:

- attitudes, e.g. *men are naturally superior to women*

- facts, e.g. *the bus leaves at three o'clock*

- feelings, e.g. *I'm angry*

- information, e.g. *I am twenty-four, married with two children.*

The essential components of effective communication are:

- an adequate self-esteem

- the ability to be an active listener

- the skill of expressing one's thoughts and ideas clearly

- being able to express one's emotions in a constructive manner

- the willingness to disclose oneself to others truthfully and freely.

Constructing a communication model

Radio transmission is a useful analogy when thinking of communication. Accurate reception depends upon the receiver being tuned in.

Between the sender and the receiver there is a gap, over which the message is transmitted. The communication gap between two people is filled with all manner of what in communication theory is called **'static'**.

Examples of communication static include:

assumptions	misconceptions
half-heard messages	values
judgements	feelings
motives	arguing
hidden agendas	criticising
put-downs	interruptions

UNDERSTANDING THE ROLE OF FEEDBACK

Effective communication cannot take place without feedback. Feedback gives both people a chance to correct the message, and helps to avoid misunderstanding.

Example
'I'm not sure I heard you accurately. What I think you said was, you couldn't come because you didn't feel comfortable meeting Joe.'

The aim of feedback is to make someone aware of:

● what he or she does

● how it is done

● the feelings aroused

● the consequences.

Guidelines for giving feedback

1. Be constructive, not destructive.

2. Check that the person is open to receive your feedback.

3. Comment only on what has been said or what you have observed, not on personality defects.

4. Comment only on what you think can be changed.

5. Be specific, don't generalise.

6. Help, do not punish.

7. Suggest, don't dictate.

8. Do not make assumptions, or explain.

9. Be specific about the effect the communication has on you.

10. Check for understanding.

Guidelines for receiving solicited feedback

1. Be specific about what you want.

2. Try not to act defensively.

3. Try not to rationalise your behaviour.

4. Summarise your understanding.

5. Share your thoughts and feelings.

6. Accept responsibility for what you said or did.

7. Try seeing things through the other person's eyes.

8. Explore the feedback, don't use it to launch a counter-attack.

9. Don't brush it off with misplaced humour or sarcasm.

10. Don't put yourself down, assuming that everyone else is correct.

11. Plan how you could use the feedback constructively.

12. If it is hard to take, remember, you did ask!

Examples of effective feedback

- 'I like you.'

- 'Your fists are clenched.'

- 'You're angry, and that's OK.'

- 'When you shouted, I felt anxious.'

- 'When you called me "son", I felt put down and small.'

- 'I'm feeling angry at what I consider to be a sexist remark.'

- 'Yesterday you said . . . I felt very angry, though I wasn't able to express how I felt. I needed to think how to say it.'

When we bring our feelings into the open in such a way as to make the other person feel that he or she is not to blame, we are giving constructive feedback, and we will be judged as effective communicators.

Effective feedback should be clear and accurate. It encourages change, because it leaves us feeling OK.

Exercise: Assessing feedback
Think back over the last week and the way you have communicated. How effective was the feedback from you and from others?

STRATEGIES FOR DEALING WITH DIFFICULT COMMUNICATION

1. Listen to the whole message – facts, and feelings, and what is implied.

2. Turn questions into statements. 'What I hear you saying is . . .' When you can paraphrase what the other person has said, you know you are listening effectively.

3. Don't argue or debate; both are futile.

4. Play Devil's Advocate, by putting the other side.

5. Addressing feelings taps into what is bugging him or her. 'You seem particularly upset today, especially when I disagreed with you.'

6. Respond with genuine feelings. 'I feel powerless to get anything done here with you, and I get angry when you try to take over by shouting me down.'

7. Agree with all that is directly relevant to the issue or problem. Agree with the individual's need to be heard and supported.

8. Draw out the motives of the other person and respond to them. Don't react to the behaviour.

USING HUMOUR

Humour is as essential to healthy interaction, to healthy people, as oil is to smooth-running machinery.

> **Those who laugh, last!**

Exercise : Making a first-aid humour box
Remember that 'laughter is the best medicine!' Suggestions for your first-aid box would be:

●   favourite humorous sayings

- a comedy record
- cartoons
- funny photographs
- riddles and limericks.

MAKING THE MOST OF SILENCES

It is as though he listened and such listening as his enfolds us in a silence in which at last we begin to hear what we are meant to be.

(Lao-tse)

- How afraid are you of silences in relationships?

- Do you fill every moment of every day with noise – anything that will fill that fearful space?

- Are you so pushed by the need to talk that you prattle on, saying anything?

- Do you use silences to be at home with yourself?

- Do you respect other people's needs for silence?

- Do you interpret all silences as hostility?

- How far can you distinguish pleasant (without tension) from unpleasant silence (full of tension)?

- How do you cope with unpleasant silences?

- In coping with negative, uncomfortable silences that are full of tension, do you:

  - argue?

  - clam up?

  - grit your teeth and keep your feelings in check?

  - blow up?

  - storm off?

  - say how you feel?

USING DIFFERENT WAYS TO COMMUNICATE

Virginia Satir identifies five modes of communication, represented by the following 'personality types'.

1.   The *Placater* is frightened that other people will become angry, go away and never come back again.

2.   The *Blamer* feels that nobody cares about him, that there is no respect or affection for him, and that people are all indifferent to his needs and feelings. The Blamer reacts to this with language intended to demonstrate that he is in charge, is the boss, is the one with power.

3.   The *Computer* is terrified that someone will find out what her feelings are. If possible, the Computer will give the impression that she has no feelings. *Star Trek's* Mr Spock was – except for the troublesome human side of him that made him so interesting – an excellent example of the Computer type. Conversing with a Computer is like listening to someone from another planet!

4.   The *Distractor* cycles rapidly among the other patterns, continually shifting the modes. The underlying feeling of the Distractor is panic, and chaos.

5.   The *Leveller* is genuine, and encourages other people to be genuine, free and honest. There are few threats to self-esteem. The Levelling response has the potential for healing and for building bridges between people. The Leveller is more likely to criticise and evaluate the behaviour not the person.

Exercise: Identifying Satir's communication modes

● What speech patterns would you identify with Satir's five modes? (You will find some suggestions in the Appendix, see page 136.)

● Can you think of at least one person you would most associate with the modes?

● Which of the five modes do you use most of the time, and with whom?

● What benefits do you think there might be of using other modes?

● Which modes would you most like to adopt?

Not being able to communicate effectively puts us at a disadvantage in establishing and maintaining relationships, and seriously affects our self-esteem, because we fail to make emotional contact with other people.

INVESTIGATING DIRECT AND INDIRECT COMMUNICATION

Indirect communication is a curse, for it relies on assumptions and obscured messages. Indirect communication is ineffective, pseudo-communication. It is manipulative and controlling, It avoids risks and is self-protective.

Example of indirect communication
Man says, 'It's cold!' then, thirty minutes later, flares up in a temper: 'You never do anything I ask of you! I wanted you to throw another log on the fire!' (J. C. Gunzburg (1997) *Healing Through Meeting*, Jessica Kingsley.)

Example of direct communication
'I want to challenge you. You say you want to be my friend, yet at least six times I've asked you out, and you've made excuses.'

Mastering direct communication

Active listening involves being available mentally and emotionally, hearing the entire message and responding in such a way that the other person knows you have heard and are trying to understand.

When we own our thoughts, feelings and behaviours, we feel more able to reveal them directly to other people. Communication means sharing views, beliefs, thoughts, values, observations, intentions, doubts, wants, interests, assumptions, strengths and weaknesses.

When we make ourselves available to others by communicating directly with them, we make ourselves potentially vulnerable; that is the risk we take of being genuine.

Identifying indirect communication

● Without direct, open communication, people cannot get to know each other. What we do not know, we will make guesses about.

● Guessing means making assumptions which are often inaccurate.

● When communication is not direct, we are forced to infer the other person's motives. Pseudo questions and clichés obscure motives.

● Indirect communication encourages game-playing, leading to deception and dishonesty.

● One of the surest effects of indirect communication is being defensive.

RESPONDING EFFECTIVELY

Listening demands an attitude of readiness and openness. There is a subtle difference between listening and hearing. Many people listen, but do not always hear.

Speech arises from the conscious mind, but non-verbal language, to a large extent, from the unconscious. To be a genuine communicator, speech and non-verbal messages must agree. Confusion results when they conflict.

Communication often breaks down when one or both people do not state their message clearly. Very often our own agenda gets in the way of hearing what the other person is saying. Being understood and understanding are both essential.

Words carry meaning, and the art and skill of communication is tapping into what lies beneath the surface. Avoid:

- asking closed questions, where a yes or no is all that is required, for example: 'You don't want to go?'

- asking leading questions, for example: 'If you were convinced that it would be immoral to do that, you wouldn't do it, would you?'

- interrogating – asking a barrage of questions puts the other person on trial.

Use open questions that facilitate communication, for example:

- What went on/happened?

- How did you feel about that?

- How did you account for that?

- How was that significant?

- What do you associate with that?

Exercise: Who do you know like this?

1. Think of people you know, and assess how many of them use indirect communication.

2. Think of your own conversations, and assess how often and in what circumstances you communicate indirectly.

PUTTING A STOP TO WORRY

Worry is a troubled state of mind brought about when we allow something to take hold of us in a relentless grip. Worry invades our whole life like a virus and destroys our peace, robs us of well-being, and decimates our self-esteem. 'But I can't help myself,' you might say. That is not true, we make ourselves worry. If outside influences control us, then we are merely automatons. Worry is a close relative of anxiety, although it does not have the same physical symptoms. Worry interferes with our sleep, and our waking; like a dog with a bone it shakes us and won't let go.

'Concern', on the other hand, means engaging or involving the mind, giving attention and showing interest. Thus concern and worry are at opposite ends of the spectrum. Worry is nearer to anxiety, mainly because worry never achieves anything; it does not involve action. Concern is more likely to lead to action.

Examples of concern and worry

● I am **concerned** that my teenage daughter, who promised to be home by ten, is not home by half-past ten.

● I am **worried** all the time my daughter is out of my sight, that something dreadful is going to happen to her, I pick up a book, and can't read. I keep looking at the clock. I can't concentrate on my favourite programme. I keep going to the door and looking out.

Estimating your worry bucket

Do you fill your 'worry bucket' with things you cannot change? Might never happen? Are they other people's problems, not yours? About the past? The future? Worry is self-communication, and starts with thought. Unless we bring our thoughts under control, they will fly around like a flock of frightened pigeons. An old Chinese proverb says:

> You can't stop the birds flying over your head, but you can stop them nesting in your hair.

Disturbing thoughts come unbidden, but we don't need to give them bed and breakfast.

Exercise: You and your worry bucket

Spend time identifying the things you fill your worry bucket with. Ask yourself these questions about each item:

● Is it realistic or unrealistic?

● Is it productive or counter-productive?

● Is it neutral or self-defeating?

● Is it easy or difficult to control?

● What would happen if I let go of that thing?

Learning to take control of worry

● Don't worry about what you cannot change.

● Don't worry about what you can change, get on and do it.

● Find a substitute for the energy your worry is using up.

● Learn to make decisions promptly.

● Learn to relax muscles that tense up when you worry.

● Learn to take little worries philosophically.

● Take steps today to start solving your problems.

● Regard yourself as a person who can rise above worry.

● Remember, it's impossible to be 100 per cent right all the time.

● Substitute a constructive habit for the destructive habit of worry.

● Write down possible alternative solutions for the worries that can be solved.

● Write down your worries. Set aside 15 minutes to concentrate on your worries. Then have a ceremonial cremation of the paper.

● Use autosuggestion to take control.

INVESTIGATING RATIONAL AND IRRATIONAL THINKING

Much of what we worry about is influenced by irrational thinking. Rational Emotive Therapy (RET) is a comprehensive method of psychotherapy developed by Albert Ellis. RET considers dysfunctional behaviour to be the result of faulty beliefs and irrational and illogical thinking.

Identifying basic principles of irrational thinking

● What we believe about past events causes problems in the present.

● Faulty beliefs continue to cause emotional upheaval in the present.

● Lasting change in our behaviour can only result from reconstructing our irrational beliefs.

Pinpointing three major irrational beliefs

1. 'I must do well and win approval for everything I do, or else I am worthless.'

2. 'If people do not act kindly and considerately towards me, they are bad people.'

3. 'Life is only worth living if I get practically everything I want without too much effort.'

Transforming irrational thoughts

As you work through the following, try to identify any which you may use, in either the form given, or some variation of it. They are adapted from my *A-Z of Counselling Theory and Practice*.

1. *Irrational*. I must have love and approval almost all the time.
   RETional. I can please some people all of the time, all the people some of the time, but I know I shall never please everybody all of the time. There are times when I will fail, I can live with that.

2. *Irrational*. Certain people are evil, wicked and villainous, and should be punished.
   RETional. People do behave antisocially or inappropriately. I would like it better if they changed their behaviour. But they are themselves and I am me.

3. *Irrational*. I feel awful when people and things are not how I would like them to be.
   RETional. I will not act like a spoiled child. I refuse to get stressed about trivial events. I refuse to say how awful everything is.

4. *Irrational*. At all times I must obey the seven great illogical Cs, and be:

   ● Cheerful

   ● Comfortable

   ● Compassionate

   ● Competent

   ● Confident

   ● Consistent

   ● Controlled.

Exercise: Transforming the seven great Cs

1. List as many situations as you can in your life where you feel you must comply with the seven great illogical Cs.

2. When you have done this, using pencil and paper, see how you could set about changing what is irrational to rational.

Something for you to think about:

> **It's not what you think you are, but what you think, you are.**

HOW I FEEL ABOUT MY MIND – PART 1

From List A select ten words, or add any word/s, which most accurately describe the **functions** of your mind.

List A
Comprehension, creativity, determination, imagination, ingenuity, intellect, intention, intuition, judgement, memory, perception, rational, reason, talent, thought, understanding, will, wisdom, wit.

Assessment of Part 1
The functions of my mind I value are:

1 ....

2 ....

3 ....

4 ....

5 ....

6 ....

7 ....

8 ....

9 ....

10 ....

Fig. 3. Assessing your mind and self-esteem.

HOW I FEEL ABOUT MY MIND – PART 2

From List B select, or add any word/s, which most accurately describe your mind.

List B

Accomplished, alert, aware, calculating, capable, clever, dense, discerning, dull, empty-headed, far-sighted, fertile, forgetful, ignorant, imaginative, indiscreet, infantile, intuitive, literate, lively, logical, mature, narrow-minded, rational, scatter-brained, sensitive, shallow, shrewd, silly, simple, stupid, unlearned.

Assessment of Part 2

The word or words I would use to describe my mind are:

1...

2...

3...

4...

5...

6...

7...

8...

9...

10...

● Now give reasons why you chose those words to describe the parts of your mind.

● How does your regard or disregard for your mind influence your overall self-esteem?

Fig. 3. (Continued).

CASE STUDY

Dave: You should know what I mean

Dave was the eldest in a family of two brothers and three sisters. Father was a morose man, who hardly ever engaged in conversation, finding refuge in his garden from a bickering wife. Dave and his siblings grew up surrounded by a negative atmosphere. Conversation was restricted to innuendo and assumptions, and such phrases as 'You should know', 'You don't need to be told', 'Everybody knows that.' Dave grew into adult life with a very low self-esteem, believing that because he didn't always 'get it right', he was stupid, something his mother consistently told him.

When Dave met and married Elsa, at the age of 22, they ran into difficulties because, although they loved each other very much, and Dave was kind and considerate, he didn't know how to converse. Elsa knew this, but thought it was due to his being shy. She had been brought up to be direct, and to ask for what she wanted. Dave, on the other hand, 'went all around the houses' before he could even hint at what he wanted. They frequently ended up in arguments.

Dave and Elsa took themselves off for counselling, where Dave was encouraged to look at his pattern of indirect communication, and Elsa was encouraged to go at Dave's pace, and to help him to learn what effective communication was. Dave was encouraged to take a public speaking course, and after a few years, proved himself an able speaker.

Exercise

Identify the main influences that contributed to Dave's low self-esteem.

SUMMARY

1.   Although talking is a natural skill, effective communication has to be learned.

2.   Communication is the cement which binds a relationship together.

3.   Effective communication rests on a healthy self-esteem and builds self-esteem.

4.   Accurate feedback is essential in effective communication.

5.   Accurate feedback should aim at enhancing not diminishing the other person's self-esteem.

6.   Feeling comfortable with silences is equally as important as talking and listening.

7. The Levelling mode of Satir demonstrates self-esteem for you and the other person.

8. Direct communication does not make assumptions; indirect communication does.

9. Worry destroys self-esteem like a rat that gnaws away at a bag of corn.

10. Controlling worry might mean reconciling yourself to the very worst that could happen.

11. Irrational thinking feeds on false premises and beliefs.

12. Transforming irrational thinking into RETional thinking could prove to be your greatest achievement.

4
Understanding your Emotions

INTRODUCTION

This chapter develops some of the themes of Chapter 3. There we saw that effective communication includes expressing our feelings accurately, particularly when giving feedback. We also saw that faulty communication is often caused by not being direct in what we say. This chapter will look at various factors which undermine our well-being and our self-esteem, namely, negative thinking; pessimism and optimism; thinking and feeling preferences; and how we exercise control over our lives.

IDENTIFYING EMOTIONS AND FEELINGS

Emotions are not identical with feelings, but they are clearly linked.

- Feelings give rise to emotions.

- Emotions are invariably accompanied by changes in the body and they influence behaviour.

- Fear, anger, love and hate are the basic emotions.

- A persistent emotion may drive a person to commit a cold and calculated murder.

- When we dwell upon positive things, we will be more likely to respond sympathetically to other people.

- When we dwell upon negative things, we will be more likely not to respond sympathetically to other people.

- When we become trapped in a loop of negative thoughts, giving rise to negative feelings and emotions, the resultant action often brings us into conflict with other people.

- Negative thinking and negative feeling are invariably linked with a low self-esteem.

- The challenge is to change negative thinking into positive thinking.

Identifying negative thinking

Optimists invariably think positively, but are often in danger of not understanding their brothers and sisters who spend their time running round in panic in negative loops. It is not a bit of good saying to a negative thinker, 'Think positively.' You might just as well tell the person to start flying. Negative thinking is often linked with irrational behaviour.

CASE STUDY

Joe: Put me down, I deserve it!

Joe's mind was consistently occupied with negative thoughts. Everything looked black and dismal. When the sun shone, it was, 'It won't last!' When his daughter won a scholarship, it was, 'We'll never be able to afford the uniform.' When his wife said she had found a job, it was, 'You'll be ill and have to give it up.'

Joe's negative thinking affected his professional life, too, although not as much as his personal life. He was an accountant in a large firm, and he was both competent and experienced. When his boss called him in, this was his thinking: 'God! What have I done wrong now? He's going to fire me. I've just taken out a loan, I'll be ruined.'

'You're looking pale, Joe,' said his boss, 'everything all right?' Joe realised he had to do something, for at that stage his heart was thumping like an overworked steam engine. He entered into a course of behaviour therapy, which helped him transform his negative thinking.

CHANGING NEGATIVE INTO POSITIVE

What Joe was doing was putting himself down by believing that everything was bad. Joe found it difficult, for example, to believe that his wife and family really loved him. So in therapy, he was encouraged to turn negative statements into positive ones. That might sound easy and simple, and that is a danger when trying to transform negative thinking. It is not enough to use a magic formula; we have to believe what we are saying.

Negative thinking and negative beliefs are so closely connected that it is difficult to separate them. For example, we saw in the last chapter that Dave grew up believing he was stupid. Growing up with this belief also affected his moods. Whenever Elsa tried to engage him in conversation, he got angry and would sulk. Part of his therapy was to re-evaluate his belief system, and determine just how his beliefs influenced his moods. If I believe I am a person of worth, then I will tend to feel confident and optimistic. On the other hand, if I believe I am less than the dust, then I will tend to be uncertain and pessimistic. Low self-esteem and pessimism tend to go hand in hand.

DISCOVERING OPTIMISM

Norman Vincent Peale, in the opening words of his book, *The Power of Positive Thinking*, says: 'Believe in yourself! Have faith in your abilities! Without a humble but reasonable confidence in your own powers you cannot be successful or happy. But with sound self-confidence you can succeed.'

Belief in oneself is at the root of optimism. A *Reader's Digest* article, 'Are you an optimist?' (July 1997), condensed from *Good Housekeeping* (January 1996), makes the following points about optimism:

1. Optimists achieve more than pessimists.

2. Optimists suffer less from depression and physical illness.

3. Optimism and pessimism are both learned approaches to life.

4. Optimists suffer as many difficulties as other people, but they are not ruled by events.

5. Optimists do not blame themselves for everything that goes wrong. They acknowledge that other people make mistakes.

6. Optimists keep on trying.

Assessing yourself
Think back to your parents. Were they more optimistic than pessimistic, or vice versa? How do you think their philosophy rubbed off on you?

Transforming pessimism
1. *Transform negative thoughts*. Every time a negative thought flies into your head, open a window in your mind and let it fly straight out. Put a positive one in its place.

2. *Imagine a positive outcome*. Don't let negative outcomes rule you. Create a positive scenario.

3. *Build on past successes*. Don't discount successful relationships, or the people that make them up.

4. *Set goals*. Without clear goals we will float like feathers in the wind.

Children who live with optimism grow up believing they were born to fly.

None of us is totally optimistic or totally pessimistic. Begin to identify those areas of your life in which you are pessimistic. You may well discover that you are pessimistic with certain people, or in specific situations. Then, using Joe as a model, start to transform one pessimistic belief at a time.

Six guidelines to building optimism

Dora Albert gives some useful guidelines for optimistic living. Her premise is that pessimism robs us of energy; and when we are functioning below par, our well-being is attacked. Her guidelines are as follows:

1. Every week, plan at least one activity you'll look forward to.

2. Expect success, not failure.

3. Plan ahead and budget your time to avoid tensions and confusion.

4. Read, memorise or listen to some positive thoughts every day.

5. Strive to maintain a serene frame of mind toward difficulties in life.

6. Learn to think independently, and to make your own decisions.

EXPLORING THINKING AND FEELING PREFERENCES

'Thinking and feeling are rival functions in the way we make decisions. Both are reasonable and internally consistent, but each works by its own standards,' so says Isabel Myers. Many of us are torn between giving allegiance to one or the other, instead of accepting that they are both necessary functions. If not trained, both functions, will, like children who grow up without guidance, become wayward.

The person who focuses wholly on thinking could become, as we saw in Chapter 3, little more than a living computer, lacking heart. The person who is totally feeling could become a bore, concerned only with sentiment and emotion. The one needs the other to act as a balance. Both thinking and feeling are essential to a healthy mind and healthy self-esteem.

Finding the right balance

We saw previously that negative thinking can lead us into all manner of difficulties, but so can feelings. Some people pride themselves on being sensitive. Sensitivity is, of course, essential in human relationships, but there is fine line between being sensitive to other people's feelings, and being touchy about one's own. In the latter case, the 'touchy' person feels the slightest breath of wind as being a slight. Against that, there is the person who could not detect a force eight emotional gale. Somehow we have to reach a happy medium.

Thinking:

● tells us *what* a thing is

● helps us understand the nature of the thing with which we are dealing

● is what we use to make head judgements

● helps us make judgements about whether a thing is true or false

● is more impersonal than personal.

Feeling:

● gives us a sense of values

● helps us make judgements about whether a thing is agreeable or disagreeable

● helps us decide to accept or reject something by determining its value to us

● is what we use to make heart judgments

● is more personal than impersonal.

People who prefer thinking (**Ts**) do not always communicate easily with those who prefer feeling (**Fs**).

Ts may feel irritated by Fs who do not approach a problem logically, and want to talk about how they feel.

Fs may feel irritated by Ts who want to analyse everything with cold logic before making a judgment.

Exercise: Deciding your preference

From the statements below, would you identify yourself as using more thinking than feeling, or vice versa?

Thinking	**Feeling**
Being rational is of more value than sentiment.	Sentiment is of more value in life than being rational.
I prefer impersonal relationships.	I prefer close personal relationships.

Being truthful is to be preferred to being tactful.	Being tactful is to be preferred to being truthful.
Analysing what people say is more essential than hearing feelings.	Being aware of feelings is of more value than trying to prove people wrong.
Being businesslike is more important than being friendly.	Being sociable is more important than being businesslike.
I like organising facts and figures.	Facts and figures don't interest me.
Judgements made with the head take priority with me.	Judgements made with the heart take priority with me.
Science and abstract subjects contribute most to society.	Good works and helping people contribute most to society.
I prefer intellectual subjects.	I prefer subjects that deal with people.

Note: This is not intended to be a 'scientific' assessment of personality.

ASSESSING WHAT CONTROLS YOU

So far we have looked at what emotions are, how they relate to feelings, how negative thinking affects feelings, and how both are influenced by what we believe. We have seen how pessimism influences thinking and looked at how possible it is to transform pessimism into optimism. The discussion was broadened out by looking at some aspects of thinking and feeling, and how both are essential to well-being and a healthy self-esteem. Now it is time to introduce what is called the **locus of control**.

Locus of control is a general term in social psychology, first introduced by Phares and developed by Julian Rotter, a Social Learning Theorist.

Internals are people who attribute responsibility for their lives to factors *within* themselves and within their control, which include:

● abilities

● efforts

● achievements

● self-direction.

Externals are people who attribute responsibility for their lives to factors *outside* themselves and outside their control, which include:

- fate
- luck
- chance
- the influence of powerful people.

Exercise: How Internal (I) are you?
How would you rate your **I** on these ten statements?

1. I have a lot of influence over my successes.

2. My misfortunes often result from my mistakes.

3. Success in business comes from good planning.

4. People generally get what they deserve.

5. Profit in business depends on capability, not on luck.

6. Being competent, rather than having the right contacts, brings recognition.

7. Preparation for exams brings success, *not* hoping for a good paper.

8. There is some good in everybody.

9. Participating in politics and social affairs can help bring changes.

10. Admitting to mistakes is a sign of maturity.

Controlling our environment
When we fail to exercise control over our environment, we do not experience the psychological success that enables us to feel satisfied with ourselves.

Externals would generally believe the opposites of the ten items listed above. If you assess yourself as being more External than Internal, all is not lost. While Rotter's work seems to emphasise the worth of Internals, Externals also have the facility of preserving self-esteem in the face of failure, and this is a desirable quality, provided we learn from our mistakes. It seems, then, that seeking control may be one way of enhancing self-esteem.

Shifting from External to Internal
Most aspects of personality can be changed. You may feel that someone who is high on the Internal score could have more to offer than you. That is a false belief and will undermine your self-esteem. You may be high

External in your private life, yet at work, or vice versa, you may believe passionately that luck plays no part in what happens. However, it is worth taking a close look at what you believe.

- How much reliance do you place on, for example, your horoscope?

- How superstitious are you?

- How much do you believe in luck or fate?

It is possible to achieve a shift from External to Internal locus of control by:

- developing self-awareness through reading inspirational books or self-analysis

- involving yourself in counselling

- developing goals

- valuing yourself through assertion training

- becoming more socially aware through group work.

When you have worked out your own control style, identify areas in your personal life, and at work, or other activity, where your style creates pressure because it does not fit with the situation or with the group.

Exercise: Analysing the locus of control
Your task is to identify which of the following statements relate to External (E) or Internal (I) locus of control. The answers are in the Appendix (page 137). Although the statements apply specifically to the work situation, most people will be able to relate to them without difficulty.

A.	Adapt well to change and new practices.	E/I
B.	Are not always reliable in the quality of their work.	E/I
C.	Believe in delegation.	E/I
D.	Co-operative, self-reliant, and knowledgeable about their work.	E/I
E.	Do not always handle delegation well.	E/I
F.	Job satisfaction tends to be low.	E/I
G.	May not always cope well with the demands of reality.	E/I

H. May not take care of equipment for which they are responsible.   E/I

I. Often have unrealistic ambitions.   E/I

J. Often rely on coercive power and threats to get things done.   E/I

K. Self-directed in their private lives and careers.   E/I

L. Tend to pick people with superior or equal ability as partners.   E/I

M. Willing to take risks.   E/I

HOW I FEEL ABOUT MY EMOTIONS – PART 1

From List A select the words which most represent the positive aspects of your personality. Arrange them in order of priority from **least value** to **most value**. You may add words which are not there.

List A
Accepting, affectionate, benevolent, caring, compassionate, empathic, enthusiastic, happy, hopeful, joyful, loving, passionate, sympathetic, tender, warm, zealous.

Assessment of Part 1
The aspects of my emotional life I value are:

1 ....   Of least value

2 ....

3 ....

4 ....

5 ....

6 ....

7 ....

8 ....

9 ....

10 ....   Of most value

Fig. 4. Assessing your emotions and self-esteem.

HOW I FEEL ABOUT MY EMOTIONS – PART 2

From List B select the words that most represent the negative aspects of your personality. Then arrange them in order, from the one you experience the most to the one you experience the least.

List B
Anger, bitterness, despair, dread, envy, fear, greed, hate, jealousy, lust, nervousness, pride, remorse, resentment, sadness, sentiment, shame, sorrow, temperamental, worry.

Assessment of Part 2
The words I would use to describe the negative aspects of my personality are:

1... The feeling I experience most

2...

3...

4...

5...

6...

7...

8...

9...

10 .... The feeling I experience least

● Now give reasons why you chose those words to describe yourself.

● Think of situations where you experience the negative aspects of your personality.

● Spend time thinking how you could change the negatives to positives.

● How does your regard or disregard for your emotions influence your overall self-esteem?

Fig. 4. (Continued).

CASE STUDY

Sean and Marie: Thinking and feeling in conflict

Sean, aged 32, is married to Marie, also aged 32. They have two boys, aged 4 and 2 years. Both Sean and Marie came to England from Northern Ireland ten years ago. Marie is a nurse, Sean a telephone engineer. They live in their own flat in London. Their marriage was starting to go through a rocky patch, mainly due to arguments. Some of the most striking differences were in the areas of Thinking (T) and Feeling (F). Marie's part-time work in the local hospital made admirable use of her F. Caring demands a high degree of F, although nurses also need T. Sean's work was mainly solitary, demanding concentration and analytical skills, although he did have contact with people when he went to repair faults. This is an extract from their comments when they came for counselling:

Sean   As soon as I come in, it's yakety-yak, like an express train.

Marie   I'm at home a lot, you know, and I never see a soul, except the boys, I need to talk to somebody. These four walls drive me mad.

Sean   Marie's scatter-brained and illogical. I can't have a decent discussion, she's all over the place, like a jumping jack.

Marie   That's true, Sean, but just listen, you never know how I feel about things. Whenever I want to talk about what's happened . . like when Mrs Cole next door came round crying, when her Billy was rushed to hospital, you never wanted to know.

When we wear our Thinking cap, everything can be analysed with logic. When we wear our Feeling cap, the heart takes over.

Compromise
They both worked hard to put on the other person's cap from time to time. Sean helped Marie to be able to think more logically, and Marie helped Sean to listen to his feelings.

Outcome
Some eighteen months later, while on holiday in Ireland, Sean proudly announced to his family that he and Marie are the perfectly balanced couple, because their personality types make up a complete whole.

Caution
Change does not work like instant coffee or tea; it demands commitment and hard work.

SUMMARY

1. Emotions are influenced by feelings, and in turn influence behaviour.

2. Positive emotions create positive behaviour; negative emotions create negative behaviour.

3. Negative thinking influences feelings, and also undermines well-being and self-esteem.

4. Transforming negative to positive thinking is not always easy, mainly because change in thinking involves changes in feelings and behaviour.

5. The roots of pessimism lie in early childhood.

6. Pessimists tend to look at the word through dark glasses, and don't have a high self-esteem.

7. Optimism enhances well-being and self-esteem and belief in one-self is at the root of optimism.

8. Pessimism can be transformed, if there is a will to change.

9. Thinking and feeling are two sides of the same coin; both are desirable and necessary functions.

10. Too much stress on either thinking or feeling can be at the expense of integration of the personality, and can lead to a weakening of self-esteem.

11. External and Internal locus of control reflect our beliefs about what influence we have over our lives.

12. Extremes of either External or Internal could suggest not facing reality.

5
Understanding what Makes Relationships Tick

INTRODUCTION

Behaviour is what we do; the way we conduct ourselves. It is like the clothes we wear which we change to transform our image. Body, mind, emotions and behaviour are interrelated, and when one is under attack, all the others are affected; well-being and self-esteem are often casualties. Relationships are an important part of life, and establishing and maintaining them is often the work of a lifetime. Two important topics in understanding relationships are attitudes and values.

UNDERSTANDING THE PLACE OF ATTITUDES AND VALUES IN RELATIONSHIPS

Attitudes affect our thinking and feelings as well as our behaviour. When we are placed in the position of being forced to change an attitude or modify a value, we feel unsettled and in conflict because the foundations of our personality are under attack. **Values** are what we consider good or beneficial to our well-being, and are therefore a vital component in our self-esteem.

CASE STUDY

Jan: William is God!

Jan found out how painful changing an attitude can be. She was a member of one of my groups, and it was soon apparent that her attitude towards me as leader was almost one of reverence. She hung on my every word, and consistently jumped to my defence when other members disagreed with me. Andy, another member, challenged Jan. 'Every time William speaks you support him, as if he can't do anything wrong.' Jan looked shocked. 'But he's the leader! He's so experienced. Of course he's right.' It took many months before Jan could begin to think about challenging what I said. Gradually her attitude changed, and she became more assertive.

Comment

Jan had been brought up in a vicarage, an only child, with elderly parents. She had attended boarding school, then went into nursing. Her whole life had been surrounded by authority figures. For her, changing that one attitude, just a bit, raised the level of her self-esteem several points.

Exercise: Identifying your values

Arrange these ten items in order of priority to you.

1. To be creative.

2. To earn money.

3. To be independent.

4. To enjoy prestige and status.

5. To serve others.

6. To do academic work.

7. To have a stable and secure job.

8. To enjoy your colleagues.

9. To have good working conditions.

10. To live a worthwhile life.

Where did these values come from? What would happen if you changed any one of them?

ASSESSING RELATIONSHIPS

Breakdown in relationships is a major source of damage to well-being and self-esteem. There is no blueprint for effective relationships. We all have to do the best we can in spite of our many limitations.

It could be argued that certain people have 'people' gifts and qualities in dealing with others. Some people do seem to have natural relationship qualities, but they also have had to work hard to perfect those skills. An analogy may point home the message. The Wimbledon star did not arrive there on talent alone; a great deal of dedication and hard slog were also necessary.

Relationships are something like that. Relationships may not be your forte but you cannot help but be involved with people. Learning about relationships is one way of increasing self-esteem. For every point won we increase the 'self-esteem-o-meter', the more energy we shall have to enjoy life, and the more other people will feel the benefit.

IDENTIFYING RELATIONSHIP NEEDS

William Schutz's theory of relationships identifies three basic needs which influence relationships and help to keep our personality balanced:

● inclusion

● control

● openness.

Identifying the need to be included

Inclusion is being *in* or *out* in relationships. It is concerned with achieving just the right amount of contact with people. Some people like a great deal of inclusion. They are outgoing, like to go to parties, prefer doing things with a group and easily start conversations with strangers. Other people prefer to be alone. They are more reserved, seldom start conversations and avoid parties.

Exercise: Assessing your need to be included

1.   In which relationships do you feel included?

2.   In which relationships would you like to feel included but are not?

3.   Which suits you better, to be outgoing or being on your own?

Identifying the need for control in relationships

Control has to do with your position in relationships. Its about being on *top* or at the *bottom*. Some people are more comfortable being in charge of everyone. They like to be the boss, to give orders, to make decisions both for themselves and for others. Other people prefer to have no control over others. They are content never to tell people what to do. They even seek out situations where they have no responsibility.

Exercise: Assessing your control in relationships

1.   In which relationships do you feel you are on top? Or on the bottom?

2.   In which relationships would you like to feel on top but are not?

3.   Would you rather have more control over others, or less?

Identifying openness in relationships

This has to do with being *open* or *closed* in relationships. Some people enjoy relationships where they talk about their feelings, their secrets and their innermost thoughts. They enjoy having one person, or at most a few people, in whom they confide. Other people avoid being open. They prefer to keep things impersonal and have acquaintances rather than close friends.

Exercise: Assessing how open your relationships are

1. How open or closed are you in relationships?

2. In which relationships are you open?

3. In which relationships are you closed?

4. In which relationships are you able to talk about your feelings?

5. How would other people describe you, open or closed?

LOOKING AT OTHER QUALITIES IN RELATIONSHIPS

Identifying the need for affection in relationships

This has to do with being *warm* or *cold* in relationships, about giving and receiving friendship. Some people want close relationships, others want distant relationships. Some want close relationships with one person, others want relationships with many people.

Exercise: Assessing your affection in relationships

1. In which relationships are you able to express the affection you want to?

2. In which relationships are you unable to express the affection you want to?

3. What are your feelings when your affection is rejected?

Identifying feelings about yourself

When we feel good about ourselves it is almost certain that most of our activities will be successful. We derive great joy from them. People who feel good about themselves:

● take risks with confidence; do not have to be either foolhardy or over-cautious

● can keep on being what they are, confident and likeable; the thought of not being liked or supported does not shatter them

- can take orders without resentment, and give orders without guilt or without fearing punishment

- can take criticism and make constructive use of it

- can take a compliment graciously without suspecting the sincerity of the giver

- can give compliments without being afraid that they will gain an advantage; do not think that others need to feel the same way about them

- can speak directly and honestly to people with whom they have a problem instead of talking behind their back.

Exercise: Assessing feelings about yourself
1. To explore your **self-concept**, examine how you perceive yourself, not how you feel about other people.

2. To understand the self-concept, you need to ask:

    - How do I behave towards myself?

    - How do I feel about myself?

3. Which of the characteristics listed above apply to you?

4. Which of those characteristics would you like to apply to you?

Identifying how available you are in relationships
This refers to being totally involved in whatever we are doing, with our total self. When we are low on availability, parts of us are scattered or detached. We are thinking of other things. When we are high on availability and identified with what we are doing, we may lose the sense of self as being different from what we are observing.

An analogy of availability would be watching a play, where it is essential to maintain emotional distance. To best experience a play, we must be detached enough to know that it is *not* happening to us, yet not so coldly detached that it makes no impression. Appropriateness means being capable of intense presence or intense detachment or anything in between.

Exercise: Assessing how available you are in relationships
1. How would you assess your availability in relationships? High or low?

2. What can you identify as being the major issues that interfere with you being available?

3. Can you identify any relationships in which you feel you are being taken over?

4. If the answer to question 3 is yes, how can you learn to be more detached?

Identifying how spontaneous you are in relationships

This refers to spontaneous expression, and is related to how much of our 'Child' we have retained (see Chapter 8).

When we are low on self-control, we become *out of control* and sometimes behave in ways we later regret. Extreme spontaneity leads to wild and anti-social behaviour. People often use alcohol or drugs to release controls so that they will be more expressive or to increase their controls so that they will be calmer.

When we are high on self-control, we feel inhibited and held back. We do not express ourselves fully. We become rigid and lack spontaneity. We are reluctant to take chances or risks for fear of what might happen.

When we are appropriately spontaneous, we do what we wish to do and stop whenever we choose to. We are able to be totally free or totally controlled or anything in between depending on what is appropriate.

Exercise: Assessing how spontaneous you are in relationships

1. How spontaneous are you? High or low?

2. In which relationships can you be spontaneous?

3. In which situations can you be spontaneous?

4. In which situations do you feel constrained and controlled?

5. How far were you encouraged as a child to be spontaneous?

6. If you feel you were too controlled as a child, how does this affect your behaviour now?

UNDERSTANDING SELF-AWARENESS

Self-awareness is about knowing ourselves or keeping secrets from ourselves. When we are low on awareness, we do not know ourselves well. It is difficult to be open with ourselves if we do not know who we are. If we are not self-aware we often behave in ways that we do not understand. We are strangers to ourselves and often do not understand why we do what we do.

When we are very high on awareness, we may begin to wallow in ourselves and to lose contact with the world. When we are too self-occupied and introspective, we may not pay attention to anything outside of self. Aware people often go through such a period but then move on to a more constructive level.

When we are aware, we know ourselves well and are aware of, and comfortable with, ourselves. We are not dark and unknown or brilliantly bright. We strive to be simply clear and open. We may be totally aware or totally unaware or anything in between, depending on what is appropriate.

Exercise: Assessing how aware you are of yourself

1.   How well do you know what makes you tick?

2.   How open are you with yourself? Or are you, even in secret, not frank with yourself?

3.   How comfortable do you feel with yourself?

4.   If you feel uncomfortable, can you track this feeling to its source? It may be a relationship from the past that is still haunting you.

Learning to use introspection as a tool to develop self-awareness

Get into a relaxed state. You may find you can do this exercise best in bed before you go to sleep.

Start with a single thought, possibly related to one period of your life. Let your mind gradually work backwards, recalling specific incidents, people, places and events associated with a particular period. Be precise. Recall colours, smells, tastes, sights, sounds and touch.

Think of a 'trigger' word, e.g. 'home', and let your mind bring every association linked with that word. Pay particular attention to the images linked with the five senses.

While doing any of these exercises, note when you allow your mind to wander. Gently bring your mind back to the last association. When the association is finished, think around those times you allowed your mind to wander and try to discover the reason why. By recalling in this disciplined way you are controlling your mind, as well as achieving insight and awareness of self.

Make your mind a willing partner, not a fettered slave!

ASSESSING YOUR RELATIONSHIP STYLE

The questionnaire below is not about 'either/or'. Rather, it is about 'more this' than 'that'. Relationship style also depends very much on circumstances. But use this assessment as a guide. When you have made your assessment, spend time considering if there are any parts of the assessment you would like to change. Then use some of the techniques mentioned in other chapters. For example, you may decide that irrational thinking inhibits your relationships, so spend time substituting RETional for irrational thinking. Use imagery to create situations in which you feel more comfortable with people. Use introspection to try to track the reasons for whatever is it that hampers you.

Questionnaire
Write 'agree' or 'disagree' against each statement.

1. Distrust of others often shows in my antagonism toward them.

2. Fear of being 'discovered' results in my establishing superficial relationships.

3. Fear of rejection and being unloved makes me anxious.

4. Feelings of mistrust are often present within me.

5. I am strongly competitive.

6. I believe in 'togetherness' as an end in itself.

7. I displace my control onto achieving power through politics or some other activity.

8. I have a strong desire to be liked, and for intimacy.

9. I have a strong drive towards self-sufficiency and self-preservation.

10. I know I can be possessive.

11. I like to be the centre of attention, and to be listened to.

12. I often feel worthless, unimportant and alienated from others.

13. I strongly desire power and to be on top.

14. I surrender power and responsibility in relationships.

15. I tend to avoid close personal ties.

16. I tend to be introverted, private and withdrawn, keeping others at a distance.

17. I tend towards extroversion.

18. Keeping everyone at a distance avoids having to show affection to one person.

19. Making the final decision is not something I feel comfortable about.

20. My inner world seems more secure than the external world.

21. My need is to influence and control.

22. My fear is of not being loved and of rejection; I feel unlovable.

23. I seek people all the time, and want others to be with me.

24. Not having others there to help worries me.

25. Passive resistance would be more acceptable for me than open rebellion.

26. The fear of being alone drive me towards other people.

27. The fear of being ignored or abandoned leads to isolation.

28. The lowest rung of a hierarchy is the best place for me, so that others take charge.

29. Treating everyone in a close, personal way is what I desire.

30. When people do not respond with intimacy I want to punish them.

Turn to the Appendix (page 137) for an assessment. When you have identified your style(s), spend time thinking through the following:

- What influences in your life helped develop that style or styles?

- How comfortable are you with the style or styles?

- What do you feel you need to change?

- What strategies could you use to encourage change?

HOW I FEEL ABOUT MY BEHAVIOUR – PART 1

From List A select the words which most represent the positive qualities in the way you relate to people. Arrange them in order of priority from **the most like you** to **the least like you**. You may add words which are not there.

List A
Affectionate, active, clam, careful, composed, creditable, decisive, democratic, discreet, fair, flexible, friendly, generous, gentle, honest, honourable, independent, influential, loving, modest, open, outgoing, placid, quiet, reliable, respectable, sincere, sociable, thrifty, tolerant, understanding, unselfish.

Assessment of Part 1

1 .... *my most positive quality*

2 ....

3 ....

4 ....

5 ....

6 ....

7 ....

8 ....

9 ....

10.. *my least positive quality*

HOW I FEEL ABOUT MY BEHAVIOUR – PART 2

From List B select the words which most represent the negative traits in the way you relate to people. Arrange them in order of priority from **the most like you** to **the least like you**. You may add words which are not there.

Fig. 5. Assessing your behaviour and self-esteem.

List B

Aloof, argumentative, autocratic, boastful, cold, dependent, disagreeable, dishonest, dominant, harsh, hesitant, hostile, inhibited, loud, mean, possessive, rash, rigid, self-centred, selfish, shy, submissive, wasteful, withdrawn.

Assessment of Part 2

1 .... *most like me*

2 ....

3 ....

4 ....

5 ....

6 ....

7 ....

8 ....

9 ....

10 .... *least like me*

● Now give reasons why you chose those words to describe yourself.

● Think of situations where you experience the negative aspects of your personality.

● Spend time thinking how you could change the negatives to positives.

● How do your personality traits influence your overall self-esteem?

Fig. 5. (Continued.)

CASE STUDY

Sean and Marie: We never go out!

We continue our story of Sean and Marie from Chapter 4. Marie was an extrovert who liked to go out a lot. Sean, on the other hand, was introverted, sociable in one-to-one interaction, but steering clear of groups. Marie's complaint, 'We never go out', wasn't quite accurate, but they certainly didn't go out a lot, and if they did it was seldom to parties but to have a quiet meal. Marie enjoyed the attention, but found it a bit dull.

Because she was the sort of woman for whom a spade was a spade, Sean frequently was on the receiving end of Marie's frustration. This became more pronounced when the children came along, and money became tight. This fact did not ease Marie's frustration, however, for her need for contact overcame the logic of the situation. Sean couldn't understand this need, for he was perfectly happy with the intimacy of their relationship, especially when the children were added.

A compromise was reached, by Marie going back to work part-time, and Sean agreeing to babysit once a week so that Marie could go dancing with a female friend. Sean was perfectly happy to study and work on his computer.

SUMMARY

1. Attitudes affect our thinking and feelings as well as our behaviour.

2. Values are a vital part of our personality, and influence our thinking, feelings and behaviour.

3. Values are what we consider good or beneficial to our well-being and self-esteem.

4. Well-being and self-esteem are damaged by breakdown in relationships.

5. Developing effective relationships is something we need to work at.

6. Schutz identifies three elements which are essential in relationships – inclusion, (being *in* or *out* in relationships), control (being *top* or *bottom* in relationships) and openness (being *open* or *closed* in relationships).

7. Other important relationship qualities are: affection, feelings about yourself, availability and spontaneity.

8. Schutz's 'self-concept' is about feeling good about ourselves and moving out towards other people.

9. Availability means being totally present with other people, as against being a thousand miles away in thought and feeling.

10. When we are spontaneous we do not feel the constraints which others lay upon us.

11. Being self-aware is not a luxury, it is a necessity, if we are to enhance our well-being and self-esteem.

12. Much of this chapter can be summed up as:
    I need to know myself, not only for myself, but to be able to relate effectively to other people.

6
Learning to Master Change and Conflict

INTRODUCTION

In several places in the previous chapters we have touched on change, or transforming something undesirable to what is more desired. Most things about our personality can be changed, albeit only a little, but that small change can make a world of difference to our well-being and self-esteem. Self-doubt can be replaced with self-confidence; low self-esteem can be replaced with high regard. The analogy used in Chapter 5 of the Wimbledon star emphasises just how much hard slog is necessary to be a winner.

DECIDING TO CHANGE – NOW

Some things we can change; others we cannot. We can remain stuck in the old groove, like the record needle, playing the same track over and over, or we can decide to change, move the needle on. At the same time, other things we can never change. Trying to change what we cannot is soul-destroying. It chips away at our self-esteem and well-being. Decide today what you can change and what you cannot. Do something about the one and accept the other.

This chapter has been written with certain implicit assumptions:

● We are capable of change.

● We resist being *forced* to change.

● We like and need to be involved in decisions and to solve our own problems.

● We avoid change because it introduces conflict, and conflict is uncomfortable to handle.

● We often prefer to stick in the comfort zone. We need to be careful, however, that the comfort zone does not turn into a steep-sided trap, out of which it is difficult to escape.

● Fear hinders change; trust facilitates change.

Assessing what you can and cannot change
In chapters 2 and 5 we looked at four aspects which all influence self-esteem: body, mind, emotions and behaviour. Look again at those different aspects and ask yourself:

1. What things about my body can I change or can I not change?

2. What things about my mind can I change?

3. What emotions do I need to change?

4. What behaviours do I need to change?

5. What is the one thing I can change that would most build up my self-esteem?

The higher your self-esteem, the more comfortable you will feel with yourself and with other people. We are only able to give love to others when we love ourselves, and when that love is continually being replenished. If our self-esteem bucket is forever leaking, we have little that is positive to give away.

UNDERSTANDING HOW ATTITUDES INFLUENCE CHANGE AND SELF-ESTEEM

An attitude is a pattern of more or less stable mental views, opinions or interests, established by experience over a period of time. Attitudes are likes and dislikes, affinities or aversion to objects, people, groups, situations and ideas. Attitudes extend into all aspects of our life. They provide us with frames of reference and affect the way we judge and react towards the people and objects in our environment.

Not all attitudes have clear-cut and obvious behavioural consequences. Mary does not approve of animals being used in circuses. If she allows that belief to influence her behaviour overtly, she may take action by organising a campaign. Her behaviour is less obvious when she chooses not to attend circuses where animals perform.

Attitudes are learned. We take many of them over lock, stock and barrel from other people. In the light of experience, some of our acquired attitudes become modified. Attitudes are determined by:

● the times we live in

● the place we live in

● the family

● the education system.

Gael Lindenfield in her fascinating book, *Super Confidence: the Woman's Guide to Getting what you Want out of Life*, gives seven essential ingredients for change. This seven-point plan is one which can be translated into our topic – attitude change and self-esteem.

Exercise: Following the seven-point plan for change
Answer these questions honestly, then decide what change you are aiming for:

Belief – do you believe that it is possible to change?

Motivation – do you need or want to change?

Insight – how far do you understand yourself and your behaviour?

Goals – are you sure your goals are your own and are realistic?

Practice – how much time and energy are you prepared to spend rehearsing new behaviours?

Support – who do you know who will encourage you?

Reward – what benefits do you want from your hard work?

DECIDING WHAT YOU CAN DO TO CHANGE YOUR BEHAVIOUR

Any learned behaviour can be unlearned. Change is facilitated through individual or group training programmes which concentrate on developing self-awareness and working towards new behaviours. Attitude change is never easy or quick. Sometimes change is painful and difficult. Where change is desired, and when it is entered upon willingly, and achieved with sensitivity, it can be dramatic and very rewarding.

A parable: Amy 'I'll get it done – sometime!'
Amy was a lovely lady, and Arthur loved her, except for one thing! Amy was a procrastinator. Her 'I'll get it done sometime' became a family joke. Amy was not into 'all this fancy stuff', meaning self-awareness. 'You should set yourself goals,' said her daughter Kate, 'then you'll get things done.' But Amy muddled on. She saw a knitting pattern in a shop window, and thought how nice the jumper would look on Arthur. She

brought the stuff home, and there it lay on her worktable, gathering various comments from her family.

This illustration demonstrates something about attitude change. We may believe it necessary, and the rewards (the finished jumper) might be attractive, but there is whole lot between the belief (buying the material) and the end. Amy would have to measure the tension (if she was that sort of knitter) to make sure the jumper would fit Arthur. She was motivated, but was her motivation strong enough? Amy had to make a start, but here she came up against her weakness, putting things off, usually because there were so many other things to do.

Nothing the family did or said changed Amy. But a remark from a neighbour did. 'My! Wouldn't that look just nice on Arthur. Isn't it his birthday soon?' Here was the motivation Amy needed. She was encouraged at the same time, so all the ingredients were there for a happy birthday.

This parable demonstrates a little of the seven points. If we are serious, then we have to make a start.

UNDERSTANDING HOW PERSONALITY INFLUENCES CHANGE

Some people see situations in only black and white terms; they cannot tolerate shades of grey.

Such people are often prejudiced against minority groups, revere authority, are closed minded, lack insight, are intolerant of ambiguity and have rigid thinking patterns. Such personality traits make change difficult. Many people do not welcome change, others positively welcome it.

The Myers Briggs personality types are relevant to different attitudes to change. In all personality work, it is unwise to say, 'this is'; rather, we should say, ' this is what might be'. Bearing this caution in mind, the following possibilities are suggested.

Extraverts (E)
Extraverts will accept change with enthusiasm, mainly because change brings with it the possibility of new relationships. If anything, the extravert may rush into change with open arms before counting the cost.

Introverts (I)
Introverts proceed with caution. Change for them brings more questions than answers, and that is unsettling.

Sensing (S)
The sensing part of us (the five senses) resists change, because it disturbs the order of things. Change creates anxiety because the blueprint, what is real, has to be rewritten, and during that stage the high S person flounders.

Intuition (N)
The intuitive part of us enjoys possibilities, revels in making the unknown a reality. For the high N person, change means new beginnings, something intuition welcomes; change energises because new worlds are there to be discovered.

Thinking (T)
Change is acceptable to 'Ts' provided it can be analysed and there is a logical outcome. Analysis requires time, so if change is hurried, before the logic is fully accepted, it will produce tension.

Feeling (F)
Change will be acceptable to 'Fs' provided there is sufficient attention paid to the 'human' aspect, and that there is ample time for discussion.

Judgement (J)
'Js' excel in reaching conclusions. Stress is likely to occur if the change process is protracted by people who can't make up their minds.

Perception (P)
Perceptive people will feel under pressure when they are forced into change, possibly under threat of some kind, and when there is a deadline to meet.

Exercise: Assessing your ability to change
From the descriptions given above, can you decide if you are more:

   E than I, or vice versa

   S than N, or vice versa

   T than F, or vice versa

   J than P, or vice versa?

In all eight types, how does your preference help or hinder your desire to change?

UNDERSTANDING HOW SELF-KNOWLEDGE ASSISTS CHANGE

Self-knowledge plays an important part in changing behaviour. Part of that awareness is being able to accept not only that we need to change, but that there are benefits from changing. Sadly, many of us are quite satisfied with the status quo, and we go all out to maintain that state, at the expense of growth. The opportunity for change rapidly passes by, and often in the passing, we leave behind a trail of damaged relationships.

God, give us the serenity to accept what cannot be changed;
Give us courage to change what should be changed;
Give us the wisdom to distinguish one from the other.
(Prayer of Reinhold Niebuhr 1892-1971)

Fig. 6. Motto to live by.

UNDERSTANDING CONFLICT AND SELF-ESTEEM

Conflict is a psychological state of indecision, where we are faced simultaneously with two opposing forces of equal strength, which cannot be solved together. Conflict may arise from within, e.g. indecision about a certain course of action, or from without, e.g. conflict between two people, or between a person and a situation.

Conflicts poorly handled can result in negative behaviours such as:

● aggression

● defiance

● forming alliances

● gossiping

● physical and psychological withdrawal

● retaliation.

Conflict resolution is strongly influenced by feelings of self-esteem. People with low self-esteem expect to be treated badly. They expect the worst, invite it and generally get it. People who do not feel confident generally feel small and, therefore, view others as threateningly larger.

Resolving conflict with other people

1. What is it you do that encourages conflict?

2. How much do you think for yourself?

3. How much do you encourage others to think for themselves?

4. How much do you try or want to control?

5. Identify your 'musts', 'oughts' and 'shoulds'. These are very controlling attitudes.

6. Who blames whom and for what?

7. What are the risks and gains of resolution?

8. Are there any possible compromises?

9. What roles·sustain the conflict?

10. What 'games' do you and others play?

11. How dominant are you? Do you always want to win?

12. What prejudices do you have that stop resolving conflicts?

Exercise: Prejudiced? Not me!

You and your spouse (partner) have decided to give a party to celebrate your promotion. You have asked a number of your respective work colleagues, including your boss and your spouse's boss. Your spouse invites a work colleague, who asks if it will be possible to bring a partner. You both agree. When they turn up at the party, it is obvious that they are a gay couple. Your boss says to you and your spouse (partner), 'I'm not narrow-minded, you understand, but I'm very surprised that you allow this sort of behaviour in your home. I run a well-respected company and I don't approve of this at all. I trust you will remedy it, now.'

How would you deal with this conflict?

AVOIDING USE OF STEREOTYPES

Stereotyping is similar to labelling, a process whereby certain negative attributes are conferred upon people or groups. Very often such people are weak, infirm, disabled or mentally ill. People of different race, colour, religion and sexual orientation are often on the receiving end of bitter stereotyping. Stereotyping people often arises from feelings of inferiority and low self-esteem. A stereotype has the following characteristics:

- It is a belief about people.

- It is a pattern of behaviour.

- It is relatively fixed.

- It is simplistic.

- It is unjustifiable.

- It allows for no individuality.

- It allows for little or no variation.

- It is often negative.

Exercise: Beliefs about other people

You are invited to consider your beliefs about the groups of people listed below. Try using the following formula: ' I believe . . . about . . . because. . .' For example, you *could* believe that French men don't respect their women folk because they are free with their sex. Don't spend long on each category. There are no right or wrong answers. When you have worked through them all, go back over them and try to identify where a particular belief originated.

What I believe about . . . is . . . because . . .

Alcoholics ....

Arabs ....

Asians ....

Blacks ....

Car salesmen ....

Catholics ....

Children ....

Civil servants ....

Clergymen ....

Conservatives ....

Doctors ....

Drug addicts ....

Fat people...

Foreigners...

Fox hunting supporters ....

French men...

Gun advocates..

Hard-rock musicians ....

Homosexuals..

Intellectuals ....

Italians...

Jamaicans ....

Jews..

Millionaires ....

Motorcyclists...

Northerners..

Nurses..

Old people ....

Police...

Polish people ....

Politicians..

Prostitutes...

Redheads ....

Smokers..

Socialists ....

The Salvation Army...

Travelling people ....

Women ....

Women as managers...

UNDERSTANDING SEXUAL STEREOTYPES

A person's gender is often the focus of stereotyped comments. Many people concentrate on the differences between men and women, invariably at the expense of considering the similarities. For most of us, being masculine or feminine is fairly central to our self-concept. In our society, men are supposed to be masculine while women are supposed to be feminine, and never the twain shall meet in the same person.

Men are supposed to be tough, dominant and fearless; women are supposed to be tender, sympathetic and sensitive to others' needs. Although it is changing, according to the traditional view, the man who is not 'masculine'; is destined to have his masculinity questioned. The woman who prefers football, and who refuses to defer to the wishes of men, is destined to have her femininity questioned.

The concept of **androgyny** refers to the blending of the behaviours and personality characteristics that have traditionally been thought of as masculine and feminine. The androgynous individual is someone who is both independent and tender, both aggressive and gentle, both assertive and yielding, both masculine and feminine, in appropriate ways according to the situation.

Much of the difference between men and women is learned rather than genetic. There is tremendous variation within the two groups. Many women behave more aggressively then some men. Many men are involved at a higher level of caring than some women. Many men never resort to physical violence; some women are violently aggressive.

Ending sexual stereotyping

1. Make a conscious choice to incorporate traits or values, associated with either men or women, if they are appropriate for you.

2. Challenge rigid sex roles which dictate behaviour.

3. Challenge sex-typing of 'feminine' women whose only function is to attend to babies and people in need, and who are discouraged from developing appropriate independent and assertive behaviours.

4. Challenge sex-typing of 'masculine' men who, in every respect, are the opposite of women.

5. Integrate characteristics of both sexes.

6. Learn to incorporate independent-assertive behaviours as well as responsible-helping behaviours. Integration helps people to be more spontaneous, for they are able to respond appropriately to situations calling for both assertiveness and caring.

Exercise: Assessing stereotypes

1. How have people stereotyped you?

2. What was said or done? How did you feel? How were you treated?

3. How have you ever engaged in stereotyping other people?

4. How did you behave towards people you stereotyped?

5. What do you conclude from these answers about the strength of stereotyping?

6. How might you overcome tendencies to stereotype people?

DON'T CARRY A TREE

Stereotyping people results from prejudiced attitudes. It is a desire to elevate ourselves by trampling on the heads of other people. It results in lowered self-esteem in the people stereotyped. High self-esteem cannot exist in heart of the person who stereotypes other people. So it works both ways. Determine today to examine your attitudes and ruthlessly root out rogue attitudes of stereotyping. The less you stereotype others, the more you will be able to challenge others' stereotyping of you. Above all, refuse to carry the burden of other people's stereotypes. Don't carry a tree when you don't have to.

CASE STUDY

Tony and Andrew handling change

Tony was a successful doctor, but suffered from an overwhelming sense of unworthiness, something that affected his relationships. He freely admitted that it was this that led him into a multitude of unsatisfactory sexual relationships. In one session, when he was talking about himself, I had a mental image of him as a small boy sitting on a dustbin. I told him, and he was moved to tears. That was exactly how he felt about himself – so much garbage, yet he gave all the appearance of a self-possessed and confident man.

Part of our work was to identify the factors that brought him to the dustbin, then work towards changing the feelings. The facts of his life could not be changed, but his interpretation of them could.

Andrew was blinded by an accident. He went through a period of grief, during which time he drank too much. Life had lost its meaning. His self-esteem hit rock-bottom. Gradually he accepted his blindness, and became a campaigner for other blind people. He is still blind. The facts cannot be changed, but his feelings towards his 'fate' underwent a change. He could not move forward until he accepted the fact that he was blind, and always would be.

Tony accepted that he could change some things; Andrew accepted that something could not be changed. Had Tony continued to kick against his past, he would have remained on the garbage bin. Had Andrew not accepted his blindness, he could have wallowed in self-pity, and his self-esteem would have suffered. His change in lifestyle brought him new experiences, and his example inspired thousands of other blind people.

SUMMARY

1. Changing aspects of ourselves is possible, but it is essential to distinguish between what can be changed and what cannot.

2. Spending time and energy fretting about what cannot be changed is fruitless and undermines self-confidence.

3. People with high self-esteem have accepted that they might not be perfect but they learn to live with themselves.

4. Self-esteem cannot be built on the foundations of self-doubt. The first brick in rebuilding your self-esteem might be to set a goal for changing something, however small.

5. Attitudes exert a powerful influence on your estimation of self-esteem. Changing attitudes requires courage and determination.

6. Following the seven-point plan provides a focus for change.

7. Don't allow your understanding of personality stop you making changes.

8. Change invariably involves conflict, either within yourself or between you and other people.

9. Stereotyping people is a potent source of lowering self-esteem.

10. The foundations of stereotyping lie in our beliefs.

11. Sexual stereotyping is an affront to people's uniqueness. You can be an agent of change if you want to.

12. Determine today that you will lay the first brick of change.

7
Assessing Stress and Self-Esteem

INTRODUCTION

In Chapter 2 we looked at anxiety. In this chapter we shall deal with stress, the signs of which relate very closely to those indicating anxiety. Stress is something strenuous and wearing which a person experiences as a result of something he or she is doing or is being done to them. Feeling tired, jittery or ill are subjective sensations of stress. Stress may arise from physical, psychological or environmental sources. It is also necessary to distinguish between acute and chronic stress. The experience of stress is highly individualised.

DEFINING STRESS

My definition of stress is 'The adverse internal and behavioural responses experienced by an individual, to one or more influences which have physical, emotional or social origins' *Counselling in Rehabilitation*, William Stewart (Croom Helm, 1985). This definition takes account of the accepted fact that there are many influences which arise from physical, psychological or environmental sources, but not all of them will be perceived as stressors by the individual. Stress is normal tension turned up several notches.

Exercise: Identifying stressful experiences
1. Identify unpleasant and pleasant experiences in your life which you feel caused you stress.

2. Then identify the various factors (situations, people) that made these events stressful.

3. Focus on the significance of the stress and on how the event affected your self-esteem.

Assessing life events as stressors

The Social Readjustment Rating Scale (SRRS) of Holmes and Rahe rates a person's lifestyle to the occurrences of certain events. They developed a scale of 43 'Life Change Units' (LCUs). The practical value of LCUs lies in the fact that people who accrue 200 or more points at any one time, over a period of about a year, are prone to physical disease or psychiatric disorder.

Life events may be accumulated over a lifetime. Unless we deal successfully with traumatic events we will accumulate intolerable stress. It then only requires some 'last straw' to push us into physical or emotional illness, or both. Stressful events of the past, together with recent stressful events, may all contribute to stress-related illness.

Exercise: Assessing life changes

This exercise assesses the 43 items of the SRRS. Rate every item with a score between 1 and 100 (where 100 indicates the highest stress levels). When you have made your assessment, turn to the Appendix (page 138) and compare your assessment with the correct scores.

Now calculate your own personal total score, based on the life events that you have experienced in the past year. If you are approaching 200, then you should take urgent action to reduce your stress levels.

Life change item	Your score	Correct score
Arguments within the home, increase in		
Boss, trouble with		
Business readjustment, significant		
Christmas		
Church activities, a significant change in		
Divorce		
Eating habits, a significant change in		
Family get-togethers, significant change in		
Family member, death of close		
Family member, gaining one		
Financial state, significant change in		
Friend, death of a close		

Health or behaviour of family member,
   concern over _____ | _____

Holidays _____ | _____

In-law troubles _____ | _____

Living conditions, significant change in _____ | _____

Marriage _____ | _____

Minor violations of the law _____ | _____

Mortgage or a loan, foreclosure on _____ | _____

Mortgage or loan, taking on one you
   can afford _____ | _____

Mortgage, taking on one that will stretch
   your income _____ | _____

Outstanding personal achievement _____ | _____

Personal habits, revision of _____ | _____

Personal injury or illness _____ | _____

Pregnancy _____ | _____

Prison or other institution, detention in _____ | _____

Reconciliation with partner _____ | _____

Recreation, a significant change in amount of _____ | _____

Residence, change in _____ | _____

Responsibilities at work, promotion,
   demotion, transfer _____ | _____

Retirement from work _____ | _____

School, child changing to a new one _____ | _____

Schooling, formal, child beginning or ceasing _____ | _____

Separation from marital partner _____ | _____

Sexual difficulties _____ | _____

Sleeping habits, a significant change in _____ | _____

Social activities, a significant change in _____ | _____

Son or daughter leaving home	
Spouse (partner), death of	
Wife (partner) beginning or ceasing employment	
Work, changing to a different line of	
Work, dismissal from	
Working hours or conditions, significant change in	

Exercise: John and Peggy's story

John was just fifty, married to Peggy, of the same age. They were approaching their Silver Wedding anniversary. John began experiencing severe palpitations, usually at night or when at rest. His heart raced and pounded, and he lay afraid to move, and too afraid to waken Peggy. He was convinced that at any moment his heart would give out. Peggy noticed how pale he was and urged him to visit his GP who organised various examinations, none of which showed any heart weakness. She advised him to see the Practice Counsellor. The following emerged:

1. John's mother had died about eighteen months before.

2. A friend had died following a coronary attack.

3. He had witnessed the death of a speaker at a conference, from a coronary.

4. He had taken on additional responsibilities at work.

5. He was studying part-time for his Master's degree.

6. Two of his grown-up children were emigrating.

7. They had recently moved to a new house, with a large garden.

8. Peggy had taken up work after a gap of many years.

Your task

● Calculate how many LCUs John had accumulated.

● What would you get John to look at?

● What strategies would you help John develop?

Turn to the Appendix (page 139) for a suggested response.

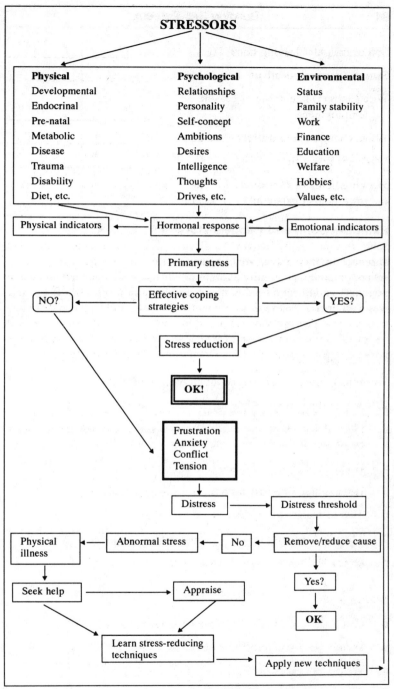

Fig. 7. A model of stress.

UNDERSTANDING THE STRESS MODEL

Figure 7 illustrates in flowchart form the causes of, responses to and ways of handling stress.

It is self-evident to say that a stressor produces stress, and almost anything may act as a stressor. If a couple are trying for a baby and one of them is proved to be infertile, there is a threat to the self-esteem of both, and the relationship is threatened; broken relationships are a potent source of lowered self-esteem. A person may be very ambitious, yet every attempt to get on results in being knocked back. The result is stress and lowered self-esteem: 'I'm a failure!'

It must be re-emphasised, that something which is not a stressor for one person can be a very powerful stressor for someone else.

Making sense of primary stress

When something (a stimulus) is interpreted as threatening, the body prepares us to confront or escape the threat (fight or flight). The signs and symptoms are as follows:

● Pupils dilate – to see more clearly.

● Hearing becomes more acute.

● Muscles tense to deal with the challenge.

● Heart and respiratory rates increase. This enables more oxygen to reach the brain to stimulate thought processes and supply extra blood to muscles and vital organs in the trunk and head. This has the effect of taking blood away from the extremities, leaving the hands and feet cold and sweaty. People would notice that the face has gone pale and the limbs are shaky.

Usually, when the threat is removed, all the bodily functions return to normal. If we are unable to turn primary stress into an 'OK' state by appropriate strategies, we will experience:

Frustration – increased emotional tension.

Anxiety – feelings of uneasiness, apprehension or dread.

Conflict – a painful state of consciousness caused by pressure of opposing forces or desires and failure to resolve them.

Tension – the feeling of unbearable strain.

If the body is not given relief from the biochemical changes that occur during the fight/flight response, **chronic** stress may result. When you are already stressed and more stress is added, the regulatory centres of the brain will tend to over-react, and keep the body in permanent fight or flight.

We cannot escape all the stresses of life, but we can learn to counteract habitual reaction to stress by learning to relax. The centres of the brain that speed up the biochemical processes when we are alarmed can be called upon to slow these processes down. The relaxation response is the opposite of the alarm response and it returns the body to its natural balanced state. The relaxation response has a recuperative effect in that is allows a respite from external stress. It keeps us from using up all our vital energy at once.

Exercise: Identifying primary stressful situations

1.   Identify the various times in your life when you have experienced the signs and symptoms of primary stress listed above.

2.   Try to recapture the event in every detail. Observe closely what is happening in your body now. This will give you an insight into the fight/flight reaction.

3.   How did you cope with the situation?

4.   Who helped you cope, and how?

5.   How long was it before your body functions returned to normal?

PERSONALITY AND STRESS

Personality influences our response to stress. Much work has been done on what has come to be called the A-type personality, and its relation to stress. The main characteristics of this personality type are:

●   undertaking more than one job at any one time, resulting in poorly done work

●   trying to cram too much work into a given time, racing against the clock

●   inappropriate competitiveness with hostility and aggression, the competitive element pervading most activities

●   a desire for recognition and advancement

● an intense, sustained drive to achieve self-elected but usually poorly defined goals

● extraordinary mental alertness.

It is reported that a high proportion of those who develop coronary heart disease (CHD) were originally diagnosed as having A-type personality. Although CHD is the best recognised stress-related disease, almost any part of the body can be the focus for stress: headaches, aching in the limbs, sexual difficulties, digestive problems.

The following factors were found to be significant in the lifestyles of men who had suffered myocardial infarct:

● a higher incidence of divorce

● loneliness

● excessive working hours

● fluid consumption

● night eating

● sleep disturbances

● nervousness

● anxiety

● depression.

Exercise: Are you a workaholic?

One of the characteristics of A-type people is that they are workaholics. Taking the characteristics listed above, how would you rate yourself on an A-type scale of 1 (very low) to 10 (very high)? If you score 7–10, then you could profitably work out ways of lowering the score and live life a little more easily.

STAYING BELOW THE STRESS THRESHOLD

Stress, if prolonged – because you have not developed effective coping strategies, or because there is no escape from it – will turn to **distress**. Imagine a 'stress tank', with a tap pouring in stressors from many sources. Eventually the level will rise and start to overflow, unless there are outlets lower than the safe level line.

Each person has a 'stress threshold'. When stress rises above that threshold, the result may be crippling anxiety, resulting in stress-related illness. When people 'crack', it is not that they are weaklings, but that their stress has overwhelmed them. We all have a breaking point. The answer is to stay physically and psychologically fit and actively seek ways of relieving stress.

> **Turn the tap off or provide appropriate outlets.**

Identifying appropriate outlets
Less appropriate outlets are: drugs; loss of temper; hitting out at people, the cat or objects; perpetual tears; and taking sick time.

More appropriate outlets are: using a problem-solving approach; engaging in 'time out' activity – take a walk, go for a run; working at a hobby; talking it over with someone else; getting it off your chest; progressive relaxation; body awareness; breathing; meditation; the use of imagery.

From the two lists given above, do *you* rely more on outlets that are less appropriate, or more appropriate? If you tend to use less appropriate outlets, how can you set about becoming more effective?

Learning to manage stress
Although much of Chapter 9 is concerned with stress-management techniques, here are ten pointers.

1. Become aware of what your body is saying to you.

2. Don't engage in negative thinking.

3. Try to express your feelings before they reach flash point.

4. Train yourself to recognise when a stressor is starting to get at you.

5. Don't imagine stressful situations that may never happen.

6. Consciously slow down.

7. Take time to relax – regularly.

8. Learn to relate positively to other people.

9. Cultivate the goodwill of others.

10. Make time to develop your spiritual life.

LEARNING TO BE CONFIDENT

Self-doubt and low esteem contribute to low confidence, and two of the common personality traits which contribute to this are **shyness** and **embarrassment**.

Understanding shyness

If you are a shy person, you have probably heard people describe you as timid, awkward, inhibited or withdrawn. Shyness rarely arouses great feelings of sympathy in other people, unless they themselves suffer in this way. Shy people generally experience intense feelings of discomfort in social situations, with blushing, perspiring and increased heart rate, some of which are indicators of anxiety. They will frequently avoid making eye contact, though this is not always the case.

Assessing your shyness levels

How many of these apply to you?

- Reluctant to initiate or maintain conversation.
- Frequent silences in which you want to crawl away and hide.
- Restricted social life.
- Misunderstood as being stand-offish.
- At work, you do not realise your potential.
- Often overlooked for promotion.
- You think your social skills are poor.
- Lack confidence to make contact with people.
- Often feel lonely.
- Afraid you will make a fool of yourself.
- Often feel guilty and ashamed without having done anything bad or wicked.

Understanding embarrassment

Embarrassment is a common social emotion of acute discomfort; the social situation may be real or imagined. It arises when we do not meet expectations, our own or other people's, as required by the situation. But we need to know the convention of which we are in breach.

Assessing your embarrassment levels

How many of these apply to you?

- Feel socially awkward.
- Often feel foolish.

- Often feel self-conscious.

- Often feel the focus of unwanted attention.

- Would do anything to escape the situation.

- Frequently imagine situations in which you are embarrassed.

- Prone to blushing and nervous laughter or smiling.

- Make limited eye contact.

- Fidget nervously.

- Don't want to look bad in the eyes of other people.

- Hate being praised in public.

- Feel overwhelmed when you witness someone making a social blunder.

- Hypersensitive to criticism.

Understanding self-confidence

Self-confidence is undermined by both shyness and embarrassment. Low self-confidence undermines self-esteem. Many people are held back by fears, yet more than half of the fears that drag us down are without foundation. Many fears come from events that have passed; you can't do anything about them. Some fears are so petty they are not worthy of consideration. If the remaining fears are real, then set up strategies for dealing with them, rather than let them rule your life.

Assessing your self-confidence

- What is holding you back from being self-confident? What can you do about it?

- How much is your life controlled by 'You have to . . .' or 'You must . . .' or 'Don't do . . .'?

- How much control over your life do you think/feel you have?

- If you feel you don't have much control, who controls you, and how?

- How often do you start something and don't complete it?

- How easily discouraged are you?

- Do people seek you out for advice or help? To ask you your opinion?

- Do you see opportunity ahead of you, or are you stuck in a rut?

- Do you persist even when things don't go right?

- How good are you at turning stumbling blocks into stepping stones to help you get on?

When you have thought about these questions, see how changing just some of them could improve your self-confidence. Here are some suggestions for what you can do to be more confident:

1. Act as if you already possessed self-confidence.

2. Assume the posture of a confident person – walk tall!

3. Become a specialist.

4. Don't get stuck in the pit of yesterday's failures.

5. Engage in social activities.

6. If you fear someone, visualise being pleasant and getting along well.

7. Know your weaknesses and your strengths.

8. Praise yourself to yourself.

9. Put yourself in the other person's shoes.

10. Seek out constructive, positive-thinking people.

11. Take a course in public speaking, or join a debating group, or take up a hobby that involves other people. You will find that the common interest helps to build your self-confidence.

Thought for the day

Remember, at a party there are likely to be others who feel shy and embarrassed, maybe even more than you are. Grab a plate and wander round offering food, and say 'Hello'. This could be your first step towards becoming more self-confident.

UNDERSTANDING ASSERTIVE BEHAVIOUR AND SELF-ESTEEM

Assertiveness is a style of communication which is clear, appropriate, not aggressive, does not show undue avoidance of the issue, is not accommodating at the expense of your own self-esteem. It does not always put the rights of the other person automatically before your own. Nor does it demand your own rights at the cost of the rights of the other person. It is a response in which self-respect and respect for the other person are demonstrated.

Assertiveness is not an end in itself:

● It means standing up for what you believe to be your personal rights.

● It means not attacking the rights of other people.

● It means expressing your thoughts, feelings and beliefs in direct, honest and appropriate ways.

● It should nurture the esteem of yourself and other people.

● It should lead to a better respect and understanding in relationships.

● It should avoid the feeling of being constantly put down and frustrated.

The goal of assertive behaviour is **direct, honest, open and appropriate verbal and non-verbal behaviour.** How often do you find yourself saying 'Sorry!' when you've done nothing wrong? Start learning to change your behaviour today.

Being assertive involves:

● Expressing both positive and negative feelings.

● Saying 'NO!' if this is what you mean.

● Being specific rather than using generalisations.

● Accepting criticism without feeling devastated.

● Accepting compliments graciously.

● Asking for what you want or need.

● Being direct instead of indirect (see mastering direct communication in Chapter 3).

● Self-awareness – knowing your goals and behaviours and the reasons for them.

● Self-acceptance – maintaining positive self-regard despite your weaknesses and mistakes.

● Honesty and openness – maintaining truthful verbal and non-verbal expression of your thoughts, feelings and intentions.

- Empathy – understanding and accepting others' experiences and feelings as valid from their frame of reference.

- Responsibility – owning your thoughts, feelings, desires, needs and expectations as well as the consequences of your actions.

- Sharing – accepting another person as equal and demonstrating willingness to negotiate issues from a win-win stance.

- 'I' messages – speaking for yourself, and not for someone else. We cannot be assertive on someone else's behalf.

- Describing the offending behaviour precisely. Not passing judgement.

Assertiveness is a dignified approach to human interaction that preserves the esteem of all parties while, at the same time, accomplishing a particular objective.

Exercise: 'I can't be assertive with . . .'

Part of learning to change behaviour is being aware of situations in which we are not as assertive as we would like to be. Situations by themselves generally do not present a problem; people do. This exercise will help you to further your self-awareness of whom, and in what circumstances, you are, or are not, assertive.

The six people I find most difficult to be assertive with are:

_____

_____

_____

_____

_____

_____

CASE STUDY

Nigel: I can't take any more!

Nigel, aged 28, was a communications NCO in the Army. His work schedule was harsh; the work was highly secret; his love life was, in his words, 'down the drain'. He wasn't sleeping well. He was moody, very angry, short-tempered, especially with his girlfriend. He just managed to keep his work together, but even there his concentration was starting to go. He felt a failure because he wasn't coping. He took an overdose of paracetamol, but gave a false name and discharged himself from hospital. He feared that if he didn't cope he would be disciplined, or worse, got rid of. 'There's no room for failures in my lot.'

When I asked him to estimate his stress level, it was 90 per cent. Not very healthy! My first task was to teach him deep relaxation. Most people when asked, 'Do you know how to relax?' will say they do, then go on to talk about activities. That is not what is meant. Relaxation is being able to progressively relax various groups of muscles so that the whole body is relaxed, and with it, the mind. My next task (although the two tasks were tackled together) was to help him express his feelings. The third task was to help Nigel get more balance into his life. This included helping him transform his thinking about his girlfriend, who, in his view, was ripping him off for all his money.

Nigel was given some strategies to use. His was listened to, and he began to take control of his life, reversing the process where he felt any control he had was slipping away from him.

If you feel life is slipping away from you, if you feel your stress levels are sky-high, you can do something to reverse the process. Start today!

SUMMARY

1. Stress arises from physical, psychological or environmental sources.

2. Stress is normal tension turned up several notches.

3. Not all stressors are unpleasant.

4. An accumulation of 200 or more Life Change Units heralds intolerable stress.

5. Whatever causes stress is likely to lower self-esteem.

6. Frustration, anxiety, conflict and tension result from unresolved primary stress.

7. Unresolved primary stress leads to distress and overload.

8. People with A-type personality are prone to stress overload.

9. Low self-esteem is linked to low confidence; shyness and embarrassment contribute to low confidence.

10. Non-assertiveness creates low self-esteem when people do not value themselves.

11. Non-assertive behaviour can be changed, but change must come from within. Changing behaviour by itself is not enough; it must go hand in hand with self-awareness.

12. Assertive behaviour is not aggressiveness, it is feeling comfortable with yourself and respecting other people.

8
Using Transactional Analysis to Build your Self-Esteem

INTRODUCTION

Getting on with people is more than just having the ability to be pleasant. In Chapter 5 we looked at what makes relationships tick. We now extend that discussion by looking at Transactional Analysis (TA), as one way of understanding ourselves and other people.

TA, a system of analysis and therapy, was developed by Eric Berne (1910–1970). TA has achieved popularity because it is relatively simple, and uses everyday language instead of the more technical and complex language so characteristic of many other psychological theories. TA lays great stress on open and direct communication, including intimacy.

IDENTIFYING EGO STATES

TA identifies three selves or 'ego states' – Parent, Adult and Child, normally abbreviated to P-A-C, and capitalised to distinguish them from parent, adult, child. Each is accompanied by characteristic verbal and non-verbal language, voice qualities and feelings. The ego states are collections of all we have absorbed from significant people in our lives – parents, grandparents, older siblings, teachers, religious leaders, and so on. Children's books often contain ideas and values which we take in. So-called 'moral' books are full of injunctions; others contain sound advice.

Exploring the three ego states
The **Parent** ego state has two functions: the Critical Parent and the Nurturing Parent.
The *Critical Parent*:

● equates to Freud's superego, and to conscience

● controls behaviour; sets limits; administers discipline, prescriptions, sanctions, values, instructions, injunctions, restrictions, criticism, rules and regulations; finds fault; judges

● is *power* orientated.

The *Nurturing Parent:*

- provides warmth, support, encouragement, love, caring

- gives advice, guides, protects, teaches how to, keeps traditions

- is in all relationships in which we felt warmth and acceptance, not being judged

- is *caring* orientated.

The **Adult** ego state functions as follows:

- gathers, stores and processes information, including memories and feelings

- is reality-orientated: decides what *is*, not what *should be*

- is objective; decides what fits, where, and what is most useful

- is concerned with all the processes that help the person develop well-being

- is analytical, rational and non-judgmental

- is a collection of all the people who have responded to us as equals, reasoned with us, shown wisdom, not patronised us

- is *rationality* orientated.

The **Child** ego state has two functions: the Free or Natural Child, and the Adapted Child.

The *Free* or *Natural Child*:

- is concerned with being creative, loving, curious, carefree, spontaneous, intuitive, perceptive, and with having fun

- is adventurous, curious, trusting and joyful

- is the spontaneous, eager and playful part of the personality

- is the most valuable part of the personality (Berne)

- is *creativity* orientated.

People whose natural child is too dominant generally lack self-control.

The *Adapted Child:*

- is angry, rebellious, frightened and conforming
- fights authority, challenges accepted wisdom, and struggles for autonomy
- is compliant, and prone to sulking
- is manipulative, protesting, submissive, placating, attention-seeking
- is *approval* orientated.

Exercise: Identifying the ego states

Ego states may be recognised by words, gestures and postures, voice tone, facial expressions. From the four lists below, identify which ego words or phrase represent which ego state. When you have finished, turn to the Appendix (page 140) for the suggested answers.

Words
according to statistics, alternatives, always, bad, beautiful, because I said so, brat, can't, cannot, check it out, childish, darling, did I do all right?, do it for me, don't worry, eek, gee-whiz, good, good, gosh, have you tried this?, have-to, how?, I never win, I see your point, I understand, I'll take care of you, I'm scared, I'm unlucky, imagine, it wasn't me, it'll all be better, it's all your fault, let me help you, let's feed the ducks, let's play, look at me now, magic, mine, must, naughty, never, nobody loves me, now what?, objective, ought to, probability, result, shan't, should not, should, smart, there-there, what will the neighbours say?, won't, wow, you'll be fine.

Gestures/postures
active listening, alert, batting eyelashes, checking for understanding, confident, consoling touch, curling up, dancing around, dejected, door-slamming, eyes rolling up in disgust, finger-pointing, folded arms, foot-stamping, giving feedback, hands on hips, head nodding, hugging, impatient foot-tapping, joyful, laughter, level eye contact, nail-biting, obscene gestures, open arms, pat on the back, pointing something out, pretending, shaking fist, skipping, striking table with fist, tantrums, thoughtful.

Voice tone
annoying, appropriate emotion, asking permission, begging, belly laughing, calm, caring, commanding, condescending, confident,

contrite, even, excited, giggling, gurgling, informative, inquiring, judgemental, loving, matter-of-fat, punishing, relaxed, self-assertive, shrieking with rage, singing, sneering, soothing, spitefulness, straight, sullen
silence, supplicating, supportive, swearing, sympathetic, tender, whining, whistling.

Facial expressions
admiration, angry frown, attentive, confident, direct eye contact, disapproving, encouraging nod, excited, eyes alert, eyes directed
upwards/downwards, flirty, furrowed brow, happy, helplessness, hostile,
lively, loving, pouting, pursed lips, relaxed, responsive, scowl, surprise,
sympathetic eyes, thoughtful, wide-eyed and curious, woebegone.

Critical Parent

Words

_____

_____

_____

_____

Gestures and postures

_____

_____

_____

Voice tone

_____

_____

_____

_____

Facial expressions

_____

_____

_____

Nurturing Parent

Words

_____

_____

_____

Gestures and postures   _____
                          _____
                          _____

Voice tone   _____
                          _____
                          _____

Facial expressions   _____
                          _____
                          _____

Adult
Words   _____
                          _____
                          _____

Gestures and postures   _____
                          _____
                          _____

Voice tone   _____
                          _____
                          _____

Facial expressions   _____
                          _____
                          _____

Free Child
Words   _____
                          _____
                          _____

Gestures and postures   _____
                          _____
                          _____

Voice tone   _____

_____

_____

_____

Facial expressions _____

_____

_____

_____

Adapted Child
Words   _____

_____

_____

_____

Gestures and postures _____

_____

_____

_____

Voice tone   _____

_____

_____

_____

Facial expressions _____

_____

_____

_____

'Childlike' qualities and attributes do not mean the same thing as 'child-ish'. The one is endearing; the other is irritating. The one makes us smile; the other makes us grit our teeth.

When we get 'hooked into' our Child or Parent ego state it is as if some unfinished business leaves that particular part of us exposed. We can never predict when it is going to happen, or who will trigger if off within us. An example will illustrate this.

I recently bought a new car; so did my neighbour. 'What do you think of it?' he asked, with pride. 'OK, I suppose, of course it's not as power-ful as a twenty-four valve one.' Mine was 24 valves! The hurt look on his face made me cringe. I later apologised, saying, 'That was a very childish remark.' That was my Adapted Child responding, feeling the need to compete; to be top-dog. Mine is better than yours!

Exercise: Assessing your ego state

From the description given above:

1. Identify who are most likely to hook into your Child.

2. Identify who are most likely to hook into your Parent.

3. How aware are you of being in either the Child or Parent ego state?

4. How conscious are you of being in the Adult ego state?

5. Who do you know who almost always acts from:

   ● the Critical parent?

   ● the Nurturing Parent?

   ● the Free Child?

   ● the Rebellious Child?

IDENTIFYING TA'S FOUR LIFE POSITIONS

I'm OK, You're not OK

The basic attitude is: 'I'm going to get what I can, though I'm not much. Your life is not worth much; you are dispensable. Get out of my way.'

Words to describe this state include: arrogant, do-gooder, distrustful and bossy.

I'm not OK, You're OK

The basic attitude is: 'My life is not worth much; I'm nothing compared to you.'

Words to describe this state include: depression, resignation, suicide.

I'm not OK, You're not OK

The basic attitude is: 'Life is not worth anything at all; we might as well be dead. So, it doesn't matter what we do or who we hurt.' Such people may yearn for warmth, but cannot accept it, and cannot trust the person who gives it.

Words to describe this state include: futility, alienation, severe withdrawal.

I'm OK, You're OK

The basic attitude is: 'Life is for living; let's live it to the full.'

Words to describe this state include: good, healthy, success, competent, confident, challenging, creative. Only this state puts people on equal terms.

Who do you know who might fit into the four Life Positions? Which of the four Life Positions do you fit into?

In general:

● When our Child feels not OK we become more used to negative strokes (see below) than to positive ones.

● When we become anxious, threatened or powerless, we have a tendency to slip back into the Adapted Child who is frequently rebellious.

● Which position we choose will depend on our particular childhood experience, and on the quality of the strokes we receive.

IDENTIFYING BASIC NEEDS

Berne's thesis is that the basic needs of social interaction are intimacy, comfort and recognition, which he calls 'strokes'. As children, strokes are physical touches of approval. As adults, we rely less on actual and more on symbolic stroking, although the need for physical contact remains strong within most people. The unit of interaction is a stroke; and exchange of strokes is a transaction.

Intimacy

Intimacy is the most satisfying solution to the need for positive stroking. To be able to enter intimacy, a person must have awareness and enough spontaneity to be liberated from the compulsion to play games (see below). Intimacy is like a harp. The music it produces comes from all its strings. Intimacy means discovering the particular harmony and melody that is enjoyed by the people involved. Sometimes the melodies will vary. Sometimes a minor key will be more appreciated than a major one. But as with music, it is all there to be enjoyed.

Stroking

Strokes, which describe the recognition we receive from others, can be verbal, non-verbal or both.

● *Positive* strokes are warm and enhance self-esteem, and evoke the feeling of 'I'm OK, You're OK'. Expressing love, caring, respect, and responding to an expressed need are all positive strokes.

- *Negative* strokes are cold and knock self-esteem and evoke the feeling of 'I'm not OK'. 'I can't stand you' is a negative stroke.

- *Conditional* strokes are given to get something in return: 'I will love you if . . .'

- *Unconditional* strokes are given without any attached strings; with no hidden motives.

We need positive strokes to maintain physical and mental well-being. Institutionalised infants have been known to die when deprived of stroking. As we grow, words are often substitutes for the physical stroking we received as children.

So often, strokes are given when we have done something. We also need strokes just for being who we are. We also need to learn to ask for strokes when we need them. 'I'd really appreciate a big hug right now.' 'Give me a kiss, darling.'

A positive self-esteem makes it in order to stroke oneself. 'I did a really good job and I'm pleased with myself.'

When we are deficient of positive strokes, our ego shrivels and we feel discomfort, and we become 'stroke hungry'. This hunger may lead us into searching for strokes at any cost. Such behaviour can be observed in some children who provoke their parents, knowing they will receive punishment, yet this at least is recognition of existence. It would seem that negative strokes are better than no strokes at all. Positive, unconditional stroking benefits both giver and receiver.

Exercise: Identifying who strokes you

1. Think back to your childhood: from whom did you receive most strokes?

2. Identify the quality of those strokes – positive or negative?

3. Who gave you the most strokes through touch?

4. From whom do you most hunger for strokes?

5. Could you ask the person for what you need?

UNDERSTANDING TRANSACTIONS

Transactions are the meat of TA. A transaction is a message from one person to another which evokes a response. The initiating message comes from the P, A or C, and is received by the other person's P, A or C.

Identifying complementary transactions

When we interact with people, we do so from one of the ego states. Indeed, we slip in and out of them all. When people are on the same wavelength there is no problem. Faulty transactions engender stress and create communication breakdown.

Request: 'John, will you help me with the washing up, please?' (A to A)

Response: 'Right, just coming.' (A to A)

Identifying crossed transactions

These create problems because something within the sender's message hooks into either the P or the C of the receiver, who responds inappropriately from that ego state.

Request: 'John, will you help me with the washing up, please?' (A to A)
Response: 'You're always on my back.' (What ego state is this from?)

UNDERSTANDING SOME OTHER TA TERMS

Scripts

Scripts are preconscious sets of rules and injunctions by which we structure our life plan. They are decided before the age of six or seven years, and are based on injunctions (see below) and attributions. They determine how we approach relationships and work. They are based on childish illusions that automatically influence our lives.

Tell me and show me

Berne proposed that the parent of the opposite sex tells the child what to do, and the parent of the same sex demonstrates how to do it.

Although injunctions (which are not always explicit, but often implied) from parents can be nurturing and conducive to the child's emotional development, they are often restrictive, reflecting the fears and insecurities of the Child in the parent. 'Don't speak to strangers' might be a useful warning, but unless that is backed with appropriate explanation it could produce fear in the child. Examples of **injunctions** are:

- Don't be yourself; be like me, or someone else.

- Don't grow up; be my little baby for ever.

- Don't be well, be sick; then I can look after you.

- Don't be a child; grow up!

- Don't be a success; you'll put me in the shade.

- Don't get too close to people; they'll hurt you.

- Don't be pushy; blend into the wallpaper.

- Don't think or feel like that (angry, sexy, happy, good); think what I think and feel.

- I know what's best for you, believe me.

Games people play

Games, in TA terminology, do not mean fun, pleasure or enjoyment. They are defences, and often cruel. A game is a set of moves with a sting in the tail.

Games allow the 'player' to collect 'stamps'. Stamp collecting is storing bad feelings to be used later. Stamps are not needed if the basic position is I'm OK, You're OK. *Brown stamps* are for negative feelings. *Gold stamps* are for positive feelings. Stamp collecting is a way of trying to help the Child to feel OK.

A game results in a sudden and unpleasant reaction (a stamp). Most games cause trouble, wrecking relationships and producing misery.

All games have their origin in the simple childhood game of 'Mine is better than yours', usually said with a lifted-up head and a superior look. As adults, we are really saying, 'I'm OK, You're not OK.' When 'Mine is better than yours' is pushed too far, the result is a punch, a slapped face or some other 'evidence' that '*Mine* is better than yours.' The example of the car given above illustrates this very well.

Examples of games

- 'If it weren't for you, I would . . .'

- 'Kick me, I'm no good anyway.'

- 'I'm only trying to help!'

- 'You never appreciate what I do.'

- 'Yes, but if you had (my husband, job, lived where I do).'

- 'Isn't life just awful!'

- 'It's all their fault.'

- 'Look how hard I've tried.'

- 'Try and catch me.'

- 'Now I've got you, you . . .!'

IDENTIFYING THE DRAMA GAME

(Also called the Rescue Triangle). The Drama game is made up of Rescuer, Persecutor and Victim.

Identifying the Rescuer role

The role of rescuer is helping, and keeping others dependent on us. In a fire, the fire-fighter is in the legitimate role of 'Rescuer', so the rescue is valid, and does not classify as a 'game'. True helping is based on the Life Position of 'I'm OK, You're OK.'

Rescuing puts the other person in the role of Victim, and implies helplessness and hopelessness, and not being able to manage without our help. We take over, thus relieving the other person of any responsibility for helping him or herself. We do it mainly because rescuing makes us feel good.

I see a blind man standing on the kerb, approach, grab him and drag him across the road, waving at the traffic to halt. Did I ask him if he wanted help? In a group situation, Jane is struggling to say something, Mandy jumps in and says, 'I think what Jane is trying to say is.' That's Rescuing. Bill, the chairman of the meeting, is being challenged by Alex; Margaret intervenes with, 'I think you're being very unkind, Alex.' That's Rescuing.

Identifying the Victim role

The Victim feels (without cause) unjustly treated. There are situations in life when a person is truly a victim; for example, having been burgled. The Victim colludes with the oppressor, does not admit to feelings of being persecuted, and does not use all of his/her own power to overcome the oppression.

Identifying the Persecutor role

The Persecutor sets unnecessarily strict limits on behaviour or is charged with enforcing the rules, but does so harshly. People who are fed up with being rescued will generally react against the Rescuer and resist any further attempt to be Rescued, or sabotage it. This eventually turns the Rescuer into a Persecutor, and will evoke this sort of response: 'After all I've done for you; all the time I've spent on you: all the money I've given you; look at you, still the same. I wash my hands of you.'

Don't Rescue me!

If we don't want to be a Victim, we must demand not to be Rescued. We may have to repeat our demand many times, because people who are confirmed Rescuers are determined, and experience tremendous feelings of guilt about being deprived of the Rescuing role.

● Think of the situations you are or have been intimately involved with.

● Identify the three roles of Rescuer, Victim and Persecutor.

● What role do you most occupy?

DON'T LET ROLES AND EXPECTATIONS TRAP YOU

We invariably become trapped in the roles we have adopted, or other people have thrust us into; for example, the good little boy – 'Johnny will always help; you can rely on him; he's always so good.' This labelling process starts early on in life. Many of the roles become traps, and if we try to escape from them we encounter opposition from others and often feel guilty.

We need to separate our own expectations from the expectations of other people. In that process we need to be very critical about what we want as our own values and roles. Are they really ours or have they been imposed on us?

When we feel trapped within a certain role, we feel stunted emotionally, and restrained. This affects our feelings of self-worth and self-esteem. So, when you are in the presence of someone, you find yourself responding from your Child, take note of the role that person expects you to perform. That might give you a clue to the hidden transactions. You may, for example, fall back into being the Rebellious Child because the other person's transaction comes from the Critical Parent, and the hidden message is: 'You be a good boy/girl, or mummy won't love you.'

Exercise: Summarising your understanding
1. You have 100 units of energy. Distribute them among your Nurturing and Critical Parent, Adult, Natural and Adapted Child ego states.
2. Into which of the four Life Positions would you place yourself:

   ● 'I'm OK, You're OK'

   ● 'I'm not OK, You're OK'

   ● 'I'm OK, You're not OK'

   ● 'I'm not OK, You're not OK'?

   What reasons would you give for your choice?

3. Indicate as many injunctions as you can which you received as a child, and from whom.

4. Identify any early decisions you made which are no longer appropriate.

5. Formulate appropriate statements which will allow you to change the way in which you are currently scripted to feel and behave.

6. Try to identify some of the games you play, including the moves involved and their consequences. Suggest an easily remembered name for each of your games.

Stop playing old tapes

Old tapes contain out-worn messages; messages from the past; messages that when we hear them immediately send us back into old behaviour. We hear, for example, mother saying, 'You can't love me otherwise you wouldn't do that.' These old tapes contain injunctions and prescriptions which control our current behaviour. What can you do?

CASE STUDY

Sally: I'll burn them!

Sally was in counselling because she felt her self-esteem bucket had nothing in it. At work (as a nurse) she was fine, but immediately she took off her uniform, she felt like Miss Nobody. Encouraged to play her inner tapes, she mentally switched on her tape recorder, not knowing what to expect. Almost immediately she heard her Mother screaming at her, and ordering her to get the housework done: she was a child of about eight. Over the years her mother berated her, put her down, called her a slut (because she was found kissing a boy, at the age of fourteen) and a moron (when she failed to get 100 per cent in her maths). Her mother was jealous of Sally's relationship with her father, and did all she could to keep them apart, to the extent of telling lies against Sally. Sally left home as soon as she was eighteen and started to nurse.

Over many months Sally worked through a range of these old tapes, even though 'listening' to them was distressing. Towards the end of counselling I encouraged her to think about how to get rid of those tapes. In imagery, she built a bonfire and threw the tapes in one by one, saying as she did so, 'I don't need to live by those any longer.'

SUMMARY

1. TA identifies three ego states: Parent, Adult and Child.

2. Each ego state is accompanied by characteristic verbal and body language, voice qualities and feelings.

3. The Parent ego state has two functions: the Critical Parent and the Nurturing Parent.

4. The Child ego state has two functions: the Free or Natural Child, and the Adapted Child.

5. TA identifies four Life Positions:

   ● I'm OK, You're OK

   ● I'm OK, You're not OK

   ● I'm not OK, You're OK

   ● I'm not OK, You're not OK.

6. Positive, unconditional strokes are essential for healthy emotional development.

7. 'Stroke hunger' is caused by lack of positive strokes.

8. Transactions may be complementary, which facilitate positive inter-action, or crossed, which lead to a breakdown in communication.

9. Scripts are sets of rules laid down in early childhood and continue to influence life.

10. People indulge in (unconscious) games in order to help the Child feel OK.

11. The Drama Game is a triangular relationship of Rescuer, Victim and Persecutor.

12. Roles are related to old tapes which keep us repeating outdated behaviours.

9
Using Strategies to Build your Self-Esteem

INTRODUCTION

In the previous chapters we have looked at several strategies, as well as exercises and questionnaires, all with the aim of helping you think about this rather elusive quality called self-esteem. We looked at what characterises people with low and high self-esteem, and how these states are created at an early age. However, a person with high self-esteem can have it shattered by events of life. So self-esteem is not a fixed quality; it can change and be changed. The state of our body, mind, emotions, behaviour and spirituality are all important. Neglect of any one of them will influence our self-esteem.

CREATING YOUR SELF-ESTEEM LIFE MAP

Everything that has gone into the previous chapters is geared towards self-understanding. Now is the time to draw the various ideas together in the Life Map. There are several ways you could tackle this: simply making a diary; setting out your life in strict chronological order; or creating a map – something I have done several times. The map I drew was made up of land and sea, islands, mountains and valleys, rivers and lakes, forests and deserts. I gave all of these names, such as the Sea of Tranquillity, the Valley of Despair, the lake of Contemplation, and used symbols to represent significant people, phases and events in my life, successes and failures, career, marriage, family and so on.

For example, part of the desert I included was when I spent three months in an isolation hospital at the age of six, suffering from diphtheria. This was a desert experience of separation from mum and dad and my brother. It was a time of great pain – physical and emotional. My self-esteem bucket had many holes knocked in it as my body was invaded by countless injections and enemas, and suffered enforced rest.

As I re-entered that experience, many years later, I knew I had to find something positive to counteract the massive negative feelings I had about those three months. I had come face to face with death, and this

122

near-death experience gave me a (positive) feeling that nothing in this life could ever bring me closer. Death could hold no fears for me. The second positive was that this experience was one of the influences that led me into nursing.

As you work through your Life Map – and it may take many weeks for you to do so – spend time exploring how that experience, that relationship, that event influenced your self-esteem. Don't be surprised if you find yourself in tears; looking over the past can be traumatic. But remember, your task is to build your self-esteem, and if that means tears, then let them be tears of healing, not of self-pity.

If you can turn your negative experiences around and find something positive, then you are not allowing your past to control you now. Only the false optimist and the untruthful will say that life has had no failures; but failure and success are two parts of the whole. We can live on failure and starve emotionally, or we can turn failure over and find something positive in it. The choice is yours.

When you have created your Life Map, review your responses and any notes that you have made relating to self-esteem or self-doubt. In a few paragraphs, state what changes you plan to make, and the specific steps that you will take during the next months to begin to advance this plan. Keep in mind that you are a product of what you inherited and past experiences, all of which influence you as you are now. By examining yourself and your environment calmly and thoroughly, you can achieve a grasp of your alternatives and take action to build your self-esteem.

USING IMAGINATION TO TURN SELF-DOUBT INTO CONFIDENCE

I have to admit to being an advocate of imagination, for I have found it to be particularly liberating, both personally and for the clients who come for counselling. There is a maxim which says that what we imagine in our minds comes to pass in reality. While this might seem like pie in the sky, there is more than a bit of truth in it when it comes to making personal changes. Our minds cannot tell the difference between real experience and one that is vividly and repeatedly imagined. That is a salutary statement, for if we constantly imagine what is negative, our unconscious mind will absorb that. Conversely, if we constantly imagine what is positive, our mind will absorb that. **Make your mind a willing partner, not a fettered slave!**

USING AFFIRMATIONS TO BUILD YOUR SELF-ESTEEM

Faulty self-talk produces lowered self-esteem. Affirmations counteract negative self-talk. Positive self-talk boosts self-esteem. Changing a non-affirmation into a positive affirmation will not be achieved easily. However, if you believe you can change it, you will end up believing in yourself.

Read through the affirmations listed below, and note any that you think you would have difficulty believing *about yourself.* Go over the affirmations you cannot give wholehearted assent to. When you have done this for all the affirmations you query, choose one, and ask yourself why, and write your reasons down. Use your imagination to go back in time and try to find out why you cannot affirm yourself. Whose voice do you hear? What words are they saying to you? What figures do you see? What gestures are being used? Being able to affirm ourselves invariably has its roots in how other people approve of us, and vice versa.

- 'I am a unique person of worth.'

- 'I own everything about me – my body, mind, emotions, behaviour.'

- 'I own everything about my personality.'

- 'I own everything about my inner world.'

- 'I own my successes and failures.'

- 'I feel comfortable with myself.'

- 'I may not know all there is about me, but I don't wish to be anyone other than me.'

- 'I may want to change some things about me, but that does not make me dislike myself.'

- 'I have made mistakes, but I can forgive myself for them.'

- 'People have hurt me, but I can forgive them.'

- 'I accept responsibility for my own life.'

- 'I am an OKAY person.'

MAINTAINING PERSONAL ENERGY TO BUILD YOUR SELF-ESTEEM

Nature has endowed all of us with more energy than we need to ensure all the stresses and strains of a lifetime. If, in spite of this generous allotment of energy, you find yourself tiring easily, *you* are probably the enemy within. When our energy is depleted, we are more liable to an attack against our self-esteem. Internal conflicts may be robbing you of energy. Some people give their car more care than they give their body! Lack of energy is likely to be emotional in origin. However, before you act on that assumption, see your doctor and have a thorough physical examination.

In all activity, energy rises from a beginning to a climax. After the climax, always take a brief rest. That is the natural rhythm of life. In the Book of Genesis, we read that God, after the work of creation, rested on the seventh day. We have a good model to work to!

Below are some guidelines for developing and maintaining your personal energy in order to build your self-esteem.

Generating energy

- Expect success.

- Learn to think independently, and to make your own decisions.

- Maintain a philosophical attitude towards life's problems.

- Plan ahead, budget your time.

- Plan important and demanding tasks for your high energy times.

- Set yourself a goal of one activity you'll look forward to.

- Start every day with a positive thought.

Killing boredom

- Associate with others in fun activities.

- Be positive, happy and at peace.

- Believe that all the energy you need lies within you.

- Don't settle for the second-rate.

- Keep your mind stimulated.

- Listen to people.

- Stimulate your creative self.

Getting better sleep

- Avoid situations that leave you filled with regret and tensions.

- Do the same thing every night before bedtime.

- Don't get too keyed up before going to bed.

- Learn to relax your mind as well as your body.

- Meditation or prayer before going to bed will help to relax your mind.

- Plan variety into your day.

- Remember, nobody has been known to die from not being able to sleep.

- Within reason, stick to the same waking and sleeping hours as much as possible.

Controlling anger

- Avoid situations and discussions which you know lead to hot arguments.

- Describe the person to yourself.

- Engage in some strenuous physical activity.

- Meditate on serenity.

- Observe how other people handle their anger constructively.

- Respond as little as possible to an angry person.

- Talk to an angry person by keeping your own voice low.

- Try to channel your anger into constructive activity.

- Use a diversionary tactic to take your mind off your injured feelings.

- When you are becoming angry, think of the person as a fictional character.

Controlling mental tension

- Act in ways that leave you feeling proud of yourself.

- Allocate your mental energy to what is really important.

- Chew on positive, but realistic, thoughts.

- Don't act in ways that leave you feeling ashamed of yourself.

- Don't expect perfection of yourself or other people.

- If you are not ill, don't lead the life of an invalid.

- Live in the present, don't dwell on the past, look to the future with hope.

- Never expect to be 100 per cent free of tension.

- Remember, you control the thoughts which influence your life.

Controlling guilt

- Don't condemn yourself because of thoughts you consider to be bad.

- Don't have sexual relationships that damage your self-esteem, or hurt other people.

- Let love, not hate, direct your energies in sex, and so far as possible, in other activities.

- Seek the help of religion, or of philosophy.

- Try to avoid doing things that your conscience warns you against.

- Worship a god of mercy, love and kindness.

Embracing peace

- Ask yourself why something is affecting you the way it is.

- Expend energy constructively, not destructively; generously, not wastefully.

- Learn to transform your negative feelings into positive actions.

- Teach yourself to feel cheerfulness instead of gloom; friendliness instead of shyness; acceptance instead of judgement.

- When you are disturbed by something which someone close to you has said or done, remain calm and try to have a reasonable discussion about it.

- Whenever things get on top of you, remember that this, too, will pass.

Setting goals

- Decide your goal, think about it, and write it down.

- Identify what your greatest drives are.

- Make one of your aims to do something helpful for someone today.

- Review your goals at frequent intervals.

- Seek professional guidance on your abilities, aptitudes and interests.

- Take one step today towards a goal you have consciously chosen.

- Visualise yourself achieving your goal.

- Work out short-term, medium-term and long-term goals.

Encouraging one another

Encouragement communicates trust, respect and belief. It can assist us to rediscover our values and joys, to identify strengths instead of dwelling on mistakes, to challenge and change old patterns, and to have the courage to be imperfect! Encouragement communicates caring and movement towards others – love. Discouragement, in contrast, results in lowered self-esteem and alienation from others – fear.

To encourage one another we should:

- Value people as they are, not as their reputations indicate or as you hope they will be.

- Believe people to be good and worthwhile and act towards them accordingly.

- Have faith in the abilities of others. This enables you to win confidence while building the self-respect of the other person, as well as your own.

- Show faith in people, which will help them to believe in themselves.

- Recognise honest effort as well as honest achievement.

- Plan for success and assist in the development of skill.

- Focus on strengths and assets rather than on mistakes.

- Use people's interests in order to motivate learning and instruction.

Treading the self-help way of confidence and well-being

- *Self-affirmation*: an appreciation of personal strengths, motives, values and experiences. You can overcome feelings of inadequacy by substituting negative self-talk with positive affirmation.

- *Self-determination*: being able to take responsibility for one's life without blaming others.

- *Self-motivation*: setting goals and taking the action necessary to reach those goals by integrating your emotions and intellect with your body.

- *Empathy*: developing increased empathic regard for others is self-enhancing and builds self-esteem – theirs as well as yours.

Nuggets to live by

- We must feel love within ourselves before we can give it to others.

- Our minds cannot tell the difference between real and imaginary experiences.

- So, imagine success and not failure.

- Quality and quantity of our contributions determine the rewards we receive.

- Improving your vocabulary increases confidence to interact with people.

- Achieving a goal means being clear about what your goal is.

- Physical contact speaks louder than words.

- Children deprived of physical contact grow up to be deprived adults.

- Play out a positive self-fulfilling prophecy, not a negative one.

- The body is the channel for what is harboured in the mind.

- If you don't adapt, frequently, the rut will close over you.

- If you are still green, you are still growing; dead things have stopped growing.

- Do something no one else is willing to do, and you will be a winner.

- *Letting go* does not mean ceasing to care; it means refusing to be responsible for what other people do, feel or think.

- *Letting go* does not mean refusing to be involved with people; it means accepting that if I dominate other people I rob them of freedom.

- *Letting go* does not mean taking decisions for other people; it means allowing people to learn from their own misjudgements and mistakes.

- *Letting go* does not mean being all-powerful; it means accepting that the outcome does not rest with me.

- *Letting go* does not mean trying to change or blame other people; it means making the most of myself, without putting other people down.

- *Letting go* does not mean just taking care *of* others; it means caring *about* them.

- *Letting go* does not mean putting things right; it means being alongside other people when support is most needed.

- *Letting go* does not mean judging other people; it means allowing others to be truly unique human beings.

- *Letting go* does not mean being in the middle arranging every outcome; it means allowing others to choose their own direction.

- *Letting go* does not mean being protective and possessive; it means permitting others to face the reality of their own decisions.

- *Letting go* does not mean denying; it means accepting.

- *Letting go* does not mean nagging, scolding or arguing; it means searching out my own shortcomings and having the courage to correct them.

- *Letting go* does not mean adjusting everything to what I want; it means taking care of myself and living every day as it comes.

- *Letting go* does not mean criticising other people's behaviour; it means striving to be true to myself and helping others to become who they want to be.

- *Letting go* does not mean hanging on to the past; it means growing and living for the future, whatever the future may hold.

- *Letting go*, does not mean carrying yesterday's burdens or tomorrow's unknown burdens today; it means having the courage to live just for today.

- *Letting go* does not mean being preoccupied with molehills; it means climbing the mountain to see the view from the top.

- *Letting go* does not mean holding on to love; it means giving it away.

© William Stewart

Fig. 8. Letting go!

CASE STUDY

The cradle to the grave

This case study is about me. Most times the majority of us cope with stress, but just occasionally we don't. Stress is not restricted to any period of life. It is present from the moment of conception; what could be more stressful than being born? Even the biological fact of growing up induces stress, as the body stretches and develops. Growing up means education, and what could be more stressful? Work? The hard grind, day in, day out. Yes, there are enjoyable moments, but these are interspersed with much longer periods of stress. Then there are relationships; we want them, we detest them. We need them and wish we didn't. Marriage comes along and then children follow, and the stress meter shoots up several notches. Of course, all these life experiences bring their joys, and most of us cope with the stresses, but we never know when we might go under, and the stress rolls over us like an Hawaiian roller. What about death? How will we cope with that? Our loved ones, parents, spouse, children? Our own dying? These are the unknowns, which only become known when we experience them.

I consider myself reasonably well-adjusted, self-aware and capable. I congratulated myself on how well I coped after mother died. I was not prepared for the sledgehammer blow which fell four years later when dad died. Until then I had never experienced depression; fed up, yes, down in the mouth, yes, but not depression. I was now an orphan, albeit a middle-aged orphan, but for the first time in my life neither of my parents was around.

What helped me survive? The love of my wife; my faith, my work, and above all, the knowledge that I had coped in the past. After about three months the grey blanket that had covered me began to change and the sky began to look blue again. I thought that was that.

Ten years later, while involved in some psychodrama, I found myself re-entering that experience, and having to deal with many of the unfinished issues surrounding dad's death, and the grief and loss associated with it.

This anecdote, I hope, emphasises that sometimes we think an issue is finished, but it continues to rumble away beneath the surface. For healing to take place we might need to take courage in both hands and find out what else we can learn from it.

You may discover as you work through this book that some of the material raises issues for you which you must deal with if you are to build your self-esteem; if you are to replace self-doubt with confidence. My experience is recorded on video just as it happened, and I know that it has helped many people to identify areas in their own lives which they need to look at. May this case study, written from the heart, help you to challenge yourself. Above all, determine today to move one more step along the road towards greater self-esteem. If you are experiencing crippling stress, and the causes cannot be removed, find some way to moderate it, so that you can live life with more well-being.

SUMMARY OF THE BOOK

As you have worked through the previous eight chapters, you will have come across the 'self-esteem bucket'. Before you continue reading, can you visualise your own bucket? What is your estimate of your self-esteem? Is it higher than when you made the assessment in Chapter 2? What have you done to raise the level?

Being able to communicate effectively is an important part of maintaining a high self-esteem. But remember, communication is two-way, and however competent you might be, you cannot make other people communicate if they don't want to! Also, remember, if you have tried to communicate, and things go wrong, try not to take all the responsibility, for this only lowers your self-esteem.

Not being able to express your feelings adequately might create in you the feeling of being inadequate and useless. After all, everybody else can! Feeling useless and inferior contribute to feelings of low self-esteem, but you don't need to continue to suffer from this deficiency. You can learn to express your feelings, but doing so depends on first recognising them, then acknowledging them. Many of us express our feelings through our behaviour. Part of the process of building your self-esteem is to work with your feelings. The exercises in this book will help; you may find it constructive to think about joining a self-awareness group, where you will develop many of the skills discussed here.

Negative thinking pulls down our self-esteem. Negative thinking is a curse, and many of us curse it loudly, but still carry on thinking the worst, and blaming all and sundry for what happens to us. This implies that we are powerless, and the more we think like that, the more we convince ourselves that it is so, and always will be. Neither circumstances nor people make us powerless; we make ourselves powerless by constantly thinking so. We make ourselves unhappy, because we allow our thoughts to dwell on unhappy things. 'But you don't know my circumstances.' True, but happiness, for example, does not come from external events (including people). Happiness or contentment comes from within and shows in our behaviour. Claire Weekes says this about happiness:

It is well to remember that none of us depends entirely on another for our happiness, although we may think we do. It is not the person we love who is responsible for our depth of feeling. This feeling is part of ourselves, is our capacity to love and it stays with us despite . . .

If you are caught in the trap of negative thinking, decide to start taking control of your thinking today. If you put it off until you feel like it you may never change!

Relationships are crucial to the development and maintenance of high self-esteem. Many of us are so driven by the need for affection, for example, that we allow ourselves to get into destructive relationships which do nothing to enhance our self-esteem. Understanding what drives you could be the first step towards changing, so that relationships enhance your self-esteem rather than destroy it.

Developing self-awareness is putting your self-interest first. The more self-aware you become, the more you will find your relationships will improve. Nothing is perfect, of course, and there will always be some people you can't get along with. Some of these relationships you can jettison; others you might be stuck with. Maybe some of the material in this book will help you cope with those difficult relationships you cannot get rid of. One of the important points to remember is – make a decision about what you can change, and what you cannot.

> **You cannot change people, you can only change yourself.**

'When the pressure of life, in whatever form it comes, exceeds your ability to cope, then you are in the whole arena of stress' (Professor Cary Cooper). In my work as a counsellor I have observed that the majority of people who come for counselling have a lowered self-esteem, which is increased by their feeling of stress at not being able to cope.

It is worth pointing out again that a person may have a high self-esteem until something comes along to knock a hole in the bucket, causing a leakage. One of the most important things you can do to rebuild a damaged self-esteem is to identify the leakages, but also to identify what stress there is in your life. Learn to control the stress level, so that you provide appropriate outlets before the stress threshold is reached and you crack. Once again, you cannot leave it to other people. You are responsible for your own well-being, and if you don't look after your self-esteem bucket, nobody else will.

In Chapter 8 we explored the fascinating model of TA, and the ego states of Parent, Adult and Child. There is no doubt that most of us respond from all three ego states. The roots of the P and C are deeply buried, and however aware we might be, there are situations, and with them, people, that are almost guaranteed to hook into our P or C, when we dearly wish we could be all Adult.

Tom tried very hard to relate to his son as an equal. Ted, however, always felt in competition with his father, and often responded from his Child. His language and behaviour included such phrases as, 'You always', 'You never', 'I'm always'. This invariably hooked into Tom's Parent, and he responded with, 'Don't be stupid', 'You're being childish', 'Grow up!' Tom found it difficult not to flare up. Perhaps Ted was engaging in the game of 'I'll see what I can do to make dad mad.'

How much of this can you relate to? How much of your Child is the Free Child? I have little of the Free Child left in me; it was stamped out at a very early age by too much adult responsibility. There is a bit, though! I know my Child is rejoicing and playing when I'm feeding the ducks and swans on the river; when I'm playing with the cat next door, or watching animal programmes on the television. How about you? What does your Child get up to?

Finally, there is the Drama Game, and the three roles – Rescuer, Victim and Persecutor. The process goes something like this:

Rescuer: You need Rescuing, I'm here, I'm wonderful. I'll make everything right. That's my purpose in life. You, after all, are weak and helpless. I am strong. You can't cope; I can.

Victim: Yes, you must be right. Don't let me stop you. Here, take all my problems. You deal with them. Never mind that I feel angry at you, my feelings don't count. I shouldn't feel angry; now I feel guilty. I'll get my own back. Every suggestion you make I will reject.

Persecutor (formerly Rescuer): I'm angry now. I'll make your life a proper misery, treating me like that. I won't let you forget this, I can tell you. I hate you! Don't ever come to me for help again!

FINALE

In all of what we have discussed in this book, the message has been, in modern parlance, 'the ball is in your court.' What will you do with it? Will you continue in the way you have up till now? Will you continue to suffer from low self-esteem? Will you allow other people to continue to knock holes in your bucket until you have no self-esteem left? Or will you accept the challenge to change? The choice is yours.

The route of change might not be easy, in fact it could be incredibly difficult. But don't let the prospect of difficulty put you off. Think of the future; imagine the future; imagine what the view will be like from the top of the mountain, as you look back and see how far you have come. As the panorama stretches out before you, you can say, 'I've done it! I am here!'

But then look up, and you will see there is more; further heights to climb. Never be satisfied with what you have achieved thus far. Your life and the lives of those you touch will be the richer for all the hard work you have put in to get to where you are. May you find that building your self-esteem, and replacing self-doubt with confidence and well-being, has been worthwhile. Building your self-esteem is like building a wall – brick by brick. And may what you have achieved be the spur for others to start building their own self-esteem.

AN IRISH BLESSING

> May there always be work for your hands to do.
> May your purse always hold a coin or two.
> May the sun always shine on your windowpane.
> May a rainbow be certain to follow each rain.
> May the hand of a friend always be near you.
> May God fill your heart with gladness to cheer you.

Appendix:
Suggested Answers to Exercises

CHAPTER 3

Identifying Satir's communication modes (page 44)

Typical Placater speech

- Whatever anybody else wants to do is fine with me.

- Whatever you say, darling; I don't mind really.

- Oh, nothing bothers me! Do whatever you like.

Typical Blamer speech

- You never consider my feelings.

- Nobody around here ever pays any attention to me.

- Do you always have to put yourself first?

- Why don't you ever think about what I might want?

Typical Computer speech

- There is undoubtedly a simple solution to the problem.

- No rational person would be alarmed by this minor event.

- Clearly the advantages of this activity have been exaggerated.

- Preferences of the kind you describe are rather common in this area.

Typical Distracter speech

- I don't know what on earth to say, but I have to say something, and the quicker the better!

- I think I'll do this. No, that would be better. Better still, maybe I'll do nothing at all.

- I have so many things on my mind just now. Now, where was I?
- Dear, oh dear! I had something important to do and I can't think what it was.

CHAPTER 4

Analysing the locus of control (page 61)
People with high External scores:
B; E; F; G; H; I; J

People with high Internal scores:
A; C; D; K; L; M

When we fail to exercise control over our environment, we do not experience the psychological success that enables us to feel satisfied with ourselves.

CHAPTER 5

Assessing your relationship style (page 73)
The numbers in the questionnaire relate to the 'types' identified by Schutz.

Inclusion
Oversocial: **Very high on Inclusion** (can't stand to be alone) 6, 11, 17, 23, 26.
Undersocial: **Very low on Inclusion** (can't stand being with people) 9, 12, 16, 20, 27.
Social: Have achieved a balance between the two extremes.

Control
Dominant: **Very high on Control** (I always have to be in charge) 4, 5, 7, 13, 21.
Submissive: **Very low on Control** (I can't tell anyone what to do) 14, 19, 24, 25, 28.
Democratic: Have achieved a balance between the two extremes.

Openness
Transparent: **Very high on Openness** (I can't get close enough) 3, 8, 10, 29, 30.
Obscured: **Very low on Openness** (I don't get emotionally involved) 1, 2, 15, 18, 22.

Personal types: Have achieved a balance between the two extremes.

CHAPTER 7

Correct answers for the Life Change Chart (pages 92-94)

1.	Spouse (partner), death of	100
2.	Divorce	73
3.	Separation from marital partner	65
4.	Family member, death of close	63
5.	Prison or other institution, detention in	63
6.	Personal injury or illness	53
7.	Marriage	50
8.	Work, dismissal from	47
9.	Reconciliation with partner	45
10.	Retirement from work	45
11.	Health or behaviour of family member, concern over	44
12.	Pregnancy	40
13.	Sexual difficulties	39
14.	Family member, gaining one	39
15.	Business readjustment, significant	39
16.	Financial state, significant change in	38
17.	Friend, death of a close	37
18.	Work, changing to a different line of	36
19.	Arguments within the home, increase in	35
20.	Mortgage, taking on one that will stretch your income	31
21.	Mortgage or a loan, foreclosure on	30
22.	Responsibilities at work, promotion, demotion, transfer	29
23.	Son or daughter leaving home	29
24.	In-law troubles	29

25.	Outstanding personal achievement	28
26.	Wife (partner) beginning or ceasing employment	26
27.	Schooling, formal, child beginning or ceasing	26
28.	Living conditions, significant change in	25
29.	Personal habits, revision of	24
30.	Boss, trouble with	23
31.	Working hours or conditions, significant change in	20
32.	Residence, change in	20
33.	School, child changing to a new one	20
34.	Recreation, a significant change in amount of	19
35.	Church activities, a significant change in	19
36.	Social activities, a significant change in	18
37.	Mortgage or loan, taking on one you can afford	17
38.	Sleeping habits, a significant change in	16
39.	Family get-togethers, significant change in	15
40.	Eating habits, a significant change in	15
41.	Holidays	13
42.	Christmas	12
43.	Minor violations of the law	11

John and Peggy: suggested response (page 94)

The counsellor calculated John's LCUs as:

1.	John's mother dying	63
2.	His friend dying	37
3.	Witnessing a death (this is very traumatic, estimated at)	30
4.	Work responsibilities	29
5.	Studying (estimated at)	25
6.	Children emigrating	29

Total LCUs 259

The counsellor saw her counselling goals as three-sided:

1.   To help John understand the stress process.

2.   To help John develop strategies for reducing his stress levels.

3.   To help John work through his feelings of grief and loss.

She explained the fight-flight response of the body, and taught John some relaxation techniques. This helped John to take control of his life and not to be ruled by his many activities.

Over several months she helped John express his feelings of loss related to:

● the death of his mother, and the subsequent responsibility for his father

● the death of his friend, and the anxiety he felt about a heart attack

● the trauma of the death at the conference, and the feelings of help-lessness and fear

● the impending departure of his two children.

CHAPTER 8

Identifying the ego states – suggested answers (page 109)
Critical Parent

Words: Always, never, should, should not, must, ought-to, have-to, cannot, good, bad, because I said so, brat, childish, naughty, now what, ought to, what will the neighbours say?

Gestures/postures: Eyes rolling up in disgust, finger-pointing, folded arms, impatient foot-tapping, hands on hips, striking table with fist, shaking fist.

Voice tones: Condescending, punishing, sneering, judgemental, commanding.

Facial expressions: Angry frown, disapproving, furrowed brow, hostile, pursed lips, scowl.

Nurturing Parent

Words: Don't worry, good, darling, beautiful, I'll take care of you, let me help you, smart, there-there, you'll be fine, it'll all be better.

Gestures/postures: Consoling touch, head nodding, hugging, pat on the back, open arms.

Voice tones: Tender, supporting, sympathetic, caring, soothing, loving.

Facial expressions: Encouraging nod, loving, sympathetic eyes, relaxed, happy.

Adult

Words: According to statistics, alternatives, check it out, have you tried this?, result, how?, probability, objective, I see your point, I understand.

Gestures/postures: Active listening, checking for understanding, giving feedback, pointing something out, level eye contact, confident, alert, thoughtful.

Voice tones: Calm, appropriate emotion, confident, informative, even, relaxed, inquiring, straight, matter-of-fact, self-assertive.

Facial expressions: Attentive, confident, eyes alert, direct eye contact, lively, responsive, thoughtful.

Natural Child

Words: Eek, gee-whiz, gosh, I'm scared, let's play, look at me now, wow, magic, let's feed the ducks, imagine.

Gestures/postures: Joyful, skipping, curling up, pretending, laughter, dancing around.

Voice tones: Belly laughing, excited, giggling, gurgling, whistling, singing.

Facial expressions: Admiration, wide-eyed and curious, excited, flirty, surprise.

Adapted Child

Words: Can't, won't, shan't, did I do all right?, do it for me, it wasn't me, it's all your fault, mine, nobody loves me, I never win, I'm unlucky.

Gestures/postures: Batting eyelashes, dejected, nail-biting, obscene gestures, tantrums, foot-stamping, door-slamming.

Voice tones: Asking permission, annoying, spitefulness, sullen silence, swearing, whining, shrieking with rage, begging, contrite, supplicating.

Facial expressions: Eyes directed upwards/downwards, helplessness, pouting, woebegone.

Glossary

Affirmations. Positive self-talk. Affirmations are useful for changing a negative self-image to a positive one.

Alexander Technique. In alternative medicine, a method of correcting bad habits of posture, breathing and muscular tension, which Australian therapist F. M. Alexander maintained cause many ailments. The technique is also used to promote general health and relaxation and enhance vitality.

Assertiveness. Assertive behaviour is direct, honest, open and appropriate verbal and non-verbal behaviour. Assertiveness is a clear, appropriate response to another person that is neither passive nor aggressive. It is communication in which self-respect and respect for the other person are demonstrated. Assertiveness is where one person's rights are not demanded at the expense of the rights of the other person.

Attachment. Attachment describes the relationship between an infant and its mother or mother substitute (care giver). This early relationship is the foundation for all later relationships. *Separation anxiety* – anxiety at (the prospect of) being separated from someone believed to be necessary for one's survival – and *homesickness* – a lesser form of separation-anxiety disorder, although the feelings can be very powerful – are both attributed to disturbance of earlier attachment.

Attitude. A pattern of more or less stable mental views, opinions or interests, established by experience over a period of time. Attitudes are likes and dislikes, affinities or aversion to objects, people, groups, situations and ideas.

A-type personality. An ingrained pattern of behaviour observed in people who struggle to obtain something from their environment as quickly as possible. What they strive for is often not clear and may be in conflict with other things or persons. A-type people are rushed, competitive, aggressive and over-committed to achieving. They are often workaholics.

Autosuggestion. Conscious or unconscious acceptance of an idea as true, without demanding rational proof. Pioneered by French psychotherapist Emile Coué (1857–1926) in healing, it is sometimes used in modern psychotherapy to conquer nervous habits and to build self-confidence.

Blamer mode. One of Virginia Satir's communication styles, where the person is constantly on the attack.

Bonding. The relationship that one individual maintains with either an inanimate object, e.g. a bird with its nest, or animate objects e.g. a child with its care giver, or adult with mate. Behaviour is directed exclusively toward the preferred object. Deficiency in bonding between mother and baby leads to attachment difficulties.

Computer mode. One of Virginia Satir's communication styles, where the person only feels comfortable maintaining an emotional distance from other people. Everything is processed objectively through the mind, in the same way as information is processed through a computer.

Conflict. The simultaneous presence of opposing or mutually exclusive impulses, desires or tendencies. Conflict may arise externally or internally.

Distractor mode. One of Virginia Satir's communication styles, where the person seems constantly in a panic, and where the emotions never stay long enough for someone to get in touch with them.

Distress threshold. The level of stress above which often results in breakdown. Stress builds up until it reaches the threshold, then spills over as distress, affecting all aspects of the person's life.

Drama Game. One of the games of Transactional Analysis; a triangle of Rescuer, Victim and Persecutor.

Ego states. A Transactional Analysis term which identifies Parent, Adult and Child as parts of the personality.

Feedback. An essential mechanism in any interpersonal communication. It gives one person the opportunity to be open to the perceptions of others. Giving feedback is both a verbal and a non-verbal process where people let others know their perceptions and feelings about the behaviours of other people. Without effective feedback, communication will flounder.

Games. In Transactional Analysis terms, a game is a sequence of transactions, which generally cause trouble, and wreck relationships because the motivation is concealed. All games are variations of the childish game, 'Mine is better than yours.'

Ideal self. What we know we could be, should be or would like to be. The ideal self often conflicts with what we are, the actual self.

Leveller mode. One of Virginia Satir's communication styles, where the person communicates and behaves from a dead straight position, and where there is high congruity between behaviour and communication.

Life Change Units. A scale of 43 items which make up the Social Readjustment Rating Scale developed by Holmes and Rahe. People who accrue 200 or more points at any one time, over a period of about a year, are prone to physical disease or psychiatric disorder.

Life Map. An imaginary pictorial map to represent a person's life journey.

Life Positions. A Transactional Analysis term, developed by Thomas Harris. The four Life Positions are: I'm OK, You're not OK; I'm not OK, You're OK; I'm not OK, You're not OK; I'm OK, You're OK.

Locus of control. A general term in social psychology, which describes the ways in which we attribute responsibility for events that occur in our lives. *Internals* are those who attribute control to factors within themselves, which include: abilities, efforts, achievements and self-direction. *Externals* attribute control to factors outside themselves and outside their control, which include: fate, luck, chance and the influence of powerful people.

Narcissism. In Greek mythology, Narcissus was the son of the river god, and a nymph. Narcissus was beautiful and his mother was told that he would have a long life provided he never looked upon his own features. He fell in love with his own reflection in the waters of a spring and pined away and died. The narcissus flower sprang up where he died. The myth possibly arose from the Greek superstition that it was unlucky to see one's own reflection. Narcissistic people have difficulty with relationships because they are too caught up with themselves, and they often have a deep mistrust of people.

Persecutor role. In the Drama Game, the Victim poses a question from a position of powerlessness; the Rescuer attempts to give answers. Every suggestion is rejected; a new one is suggested, until eventually the Rescuer becomes angry, switches roles and persecutes the Victim. When we Rescue people who don't need it, we put them down, emphasise their helplessness and exalt our own superiority over the Victim who will in the end become angry at the Rescuer. Every Rescue–Victim transaction will result in a Persecutor–Victim transaction.

Placater mode. One of Virginia Satir's communication styles, where the person is terrified to say what he or she wants to say, in case the other person takes offence. There is a constant need to make everything right, and to avoid anything that might lead to conflict, however minor.

Primary stress. Normal tensions in life produce primary stress, in which we experience physical and emotional indicators of anxiety. If we cope satisfactorily our bodily functions return to normal. If stress is piled on, the coping mechanisms cease to be effective and we are in danger of developing distress, or stress overload.

Psyche. Named after the Greek heroine who fell in love with Cupid. Represented in art as a butterfly. In psychology, it is the centre of thought, feeling and behaviour, which, consciously or unconsciously, adjusts and relates the body to its social and physical environment.

Psychosynthesis. A synonym for human growth, the ongoing process of integrating all the parts, aspects and energies of the individual into a harmonious, powerful whole. Psychosynthesis was developed by Assagioli, an Italian psychiatrist who broke away from Freudian orthodoxy early this century and developed an integrated approach to psychiatry. It draws upon psychoanalysis, Jungian and existential psychology, Buddhism, Yoga and Christian traditions and philosophies.

Rescuer role. One of the roles in the Drama Game. The Rescuer views the Victim as being helpless and powerless, and in need of being Rescued. The result is to increase the Victim's sense of powerlessness.

RET. A comprehensive method of psychotherapy developed by Albert Ellis. RET considers dysfunctional behaviour to be the result of faulty beliefs and irrational and illogical thinking. The method has elements in common with both cognitive and behavioural therapy.

Self-concept. The composite of ideas, feelings and attitudes which we have about ourselves. It is the centre of our personal universe; our frame of reference; our personal reality; a screen through which we see, hear, evaluate and understand. People with weak self-concepts distort the way they think others perceive them. They fear that disagreeing with others may give the impression of not liking them. People with weak self-concepts may have difficulty: communicating with others; admitting that they are wrong; expressing feelings – positive or negative; accepting criticism; voicing ideas that are different from those held by other people.

Self-esteem. A confidence and satisfaction in oneself, self-respect. Self-esteem is the value we place on ourselves. A high self-esteem is a positive value; a low self-esteem results from attaching negative values to ourselves or some part of ourselves.

Stereotype. Stereotyping is a behaviour that classifies groups of people, generally in unfavourable terms. Stereotyping puts people down, because it attributes to them all the characteristics which we have observed in only a few. Stereotyping lumps everybody together; this has come to be known as the halo effect – a tendency to allow an overall impression of a person or one particular outstanding trait to influence the total impression of that person.

Stress. The adverse internal and behavioural responses experienced by an individual, to one or more influences which have physical, emotional or social origins. Stress is something strenuous and wearing which a person experiences as a result of something he or she is doing or is being done to them. Feeling tired, jittery or ill are subjective sensations of stress. When the pressure of life, in whatever form it comes, exceeds our ability to cope, then we are in the whole arena of stress.

Strokes. A Transactional Analysis term to denote the recognition we receive from other people. Strokes may be positive, negative, conditional or unconditional. We need positive strokes to maintain physical and mental well-being, and to develop a healthy self-esteem.

Transactional Analysis (TA). A system of analysis and therapy developed by Berne. The theoretical framework comprises:

- various 'selves' or ego states – Parent, Adult, Child – which form the personality

- transactions between people and between one's various selves

- an individual existential position

- a preconscious life-plan or 'script'.

Victim role. In the Drama Game, the Victim plays the role of the helpless person who needs someone strong to act as Rescuer. The more this happens, the more the unequal position is emphasised. When the Victim has had enough, he or she may, like the proverbial worm, turn, and refuse any more Rescuing, thus forcing the Rescuer to become the Persecutor.

Further Reading

Further Reading

Assert Yourself, R. Sharpe (Kogan Page, 1989).

Attachment, J. Bowlby (Penguin, 1969).

A Woman In Your Own Right, A. Dickson (Quartet Books, 1982).

A–Z of Counselling Theory and Practice, William Stewart (Stanley Thornes, 1997, 2nd edition).

Concentration: An Approach to Meditation, (The Theosophical Publishing House, 1985).

Courage and Confidence, Norman Vincent Peale (Cedar, 1992).

Games People Play, E. Berne (Grove Press, 1964).

Gifts Differing, Isabel Myers Briggs (Consultant Psychologist Press, 1980).

How to Stop Worrying and Start Living, Dale Carnegie (The World's Work Ltd, 1948, and edited by Dorothy Carnegie, 1990).

How to Win Friends and Influence People, Dale Carnegie (Cedar, revised edition 1986).

Human Relationship Skills, R. Nelson-Jones (Holt, Rinehart and Winston, 1986).

Imagery and Symbolism in Counselling, William Stewart (Jessica Kingsley, 1996).

I'm OK – You're OK, Thomas A. Harris (Harper and Row, 1969).

Influencing with Integrity, G. Z. Laborde (Syntony Publishing, 1987).

Interpersonal Underworld, William Schutz (Science and Behaviour Books, 1966).

Learning to Counsel: How to Develop the Skills to Work Effectively with Others, Jan Sutton and William Stewart (How To Books, 1997).

Peoplemaking, Virginia Satir (Science and Behaviour Books, 1972).

Please Understand Me, David Keirsey and Marilyn Bates (Prometheus Nemesis Book, 1984). Kiersey provides a detailed self-scoring questionnaire.

Prescription for Anxiety, Leslie D. Weatherhead (Hodder and Stoughton, 1956).

Psychosynthesis, Roberto Assagioli (Turnstone Books, 1965).

Seeds of Greatness, Denis Waitley (Cedar, 1987).

Self-Esteem, Gael Lindenfield (Thorsons, 1995).

Self-Esteem, Virginia Satir (Celestial Arts, 1975).

Self Help for your Nerves, Claire Weekes (Angus and Robertson Publishers, 1962).

Stop Feeling Tired and Start Living, Dora Albert (A. Thomas & Co., 1960).

Stressmaster, Richard Terry Lovelace (John Wiley & Sons, 1990).

Super Confidence: the Woman's Guide to Getting what you Want out of Life, Gael Lindenfield (Thorsons, 1989).

TA Today, I Stewart & V. Joines (Lifespace Publishing, 1987).

Thriving on Stress: How to Manage Pressures and Transform Your Life, Jan Sutton (How To Books, 1998).

The Power of Positive Thinking, Norman Vincent Peale (Cedar, 1953).

The Psychology of Consciousness, R. E. Ornstein (Pelican, 1975).

The Relaxation and Stress Reduction Workbook, Martha Davis, Elizabeth Robbins Eshelman, Matthew McKay (New Harbinger Publications, 1982).

The Self-Esteem Workbook: an Interactive Approach to Changing your Life, Lynda Field (Element, 1995).

'The Social Readjustment Rating Scale', T. H. Holmes and R. H. Rahe *(Journal of Psychosomatic Research*, Vol. 8, 1967, page 35).

The Stress of Life, H. Selye (Longman, Green & Co., 1957).

Use Both Sides of Your Brain, T. Buzan (E. P. Dutton, 1983).

Useful Addresses

The Institute of Counselling, 6 Dixon Street, Glasgow. G1 4AX. Tel: (0141) 204 2230. Fax: (0141) 221 2841. Website: www.collegeofcounselling.co.uk. In addition to many different distance learning counselling courses, the Institute runs an Introduction to Stress Management course, part of which is a Relaxation Instruction tape, produced by William Stewart.

British Association for Counselling, 1 Regent Place, Rugby, Warwickshire CV21 2PJ. Tel: (01788) 550899. Fax: (01788) 562189. Website: www.counselling.co.uk. The BAC produces a directory of counsellors and their particular interests.

Centre for Stress Management, 156 Westcombe Hill, London SE3 7DH. Tel: (0181) 293 4114. Or (0181) 853 1122. Fax: (0181) 293 1441.

Institute of Family Therapy, 24-32 Stephenson Way, London NW 2HX. Tel: (0171) 391-9150. Fax: (0181) 391 9169. Family therapy: working with families experiencing psychological, behavioural and relationship problems.

RELATE Marriage Guidance, National Headquarters, Herbert Gray College, Little Church Street, Rugby CV21 3AP. Tel: (01788) 573241. Website: www.relate.org.uk. Counselling for relationship problems: sexual problems (some branches). For local branches see under RELATE in local 'phone book.

Westminster Pastoral Foundation Counselling, 23 Kensington Square, London W8 5HN. Tel: (0171) 937 6956. Fax: (0171) 937 1767. Website: www. wpf.org.uk. Provides a professional service of counselling/psychotherapy.

The best sources for local information are:

1. GP practices who will have details of local services available.
2. *Yellow Pages* – look under section Counselling and Advice; Psychotherapy; Analysis.
3. Citizens Advice Bureau.
4. Councils of Community Service.
5. Local newspapers often provide a list of helpline telephone numbers.

Index

SELF-COUNSELLING
How to develop the skills to positively manage your life

William Stewart

Self-counselling is one way of working towards understanding yourself and others. For some people it might be a substitute for face-to-face counselling, for others a back up. In this practical self-help book, William Stewart introduces many self-counselling skills and techniques and uses case studies and exercises, working with dreams, imagination, and intuition, to develop both a deeper self-awareness and the ability to solve problems. William Stewart has many years' experience in mental health and counselling. He is author of the highly successful *A-Z of Counselling Theory and Practice*, a recognised reference book for counsellors and has written three other How To Books, including (with Jan Sutton) *Learning to Counsel*.

144p. illus. 1 85703 283 7.

THRIVING ON STRESS
How to manage pressures and transform you life

Jan Sutton

The pressures of modern life make us susceptible to stress. However not all stress is negative – if managed effectively we can positively thrive on it. Peak performance stress stimulates activity, enhances creativity, and motivates us to live happy and fulfilling lives. Drawing on her experience as a counsellor, stress management and assertiveness trainer, Jan Sutton not only equips you with easily mastered strategies for conquering negative stress, she also offers you a personal development programme for building self-esteem and self-confidence. The book is complete with comprehensive case studies, illustrations, and practical activities. Jan Sutton (Dip CPC) is co-author (with William Stewart) of *Learning to Counsel* in this series.

192 pp. illus. 1 85703 238 1.

LEARNING TO COUNSEL
How to develop the skills to work effectively with others

Jan Sutton and William Stewart

Counselling skills are not only used by professional counsellors —
they are relevant to a wide range of people as part of their work. They
can also enhance all relationships. This practical book presents the
principles of counselling and the fundamental skills involved. It is
arranged in a logical sequence with exercises to work through and case
studies to follow throughout the book. Jan Sutton (Dip CPC) is an
independent counsellor, trainer, author and personal development consultant. She facilitates counselling and related topics for the University
of Southampton and various adult education departments. William
Stewart is a freelance counsellor, counsellor supervisor, and author
whose background is nursing, psychiatric social work and four years as
a student counsellor/lecturer.

160pp. illus. 1 85703 229 2.

UNLOCKING YOUR POTENTIAL
How to master your mind, life and destiny

Peter Marshall

Even the smartest individuals will not fulfil their potential on intellect
alone; first they must free themselves from their own limiting expectations. If you really want to become master of your own life you will
need to remove the barriers to success. This book will show you how
to do it. It will introduce you to objective techniques for overcoming
the limiting effects of the past: conditioning, misguided or obsolete
teachings, repressed conflicts and the expectations imposed on us by
others. Peter Marshall is a research psychologist, who specialises in
mind and memory, and is a member of the Applied Psychology
Research Group of the University of London. He is author of *How To
Study and Learn* and *Research Methods* in this series.

144p. 1 85703 252 7.

MAXIMISING YOUR MEMORY
How to train yourself to remember more

Peter Marshall

A powerful memory brings obvious advantages in educational, career and social terms. At school and college those certificates which provide a passport to a career depend heavily on what you can remember in the exam room. In the world of work, being able to recall details which slip the minds of colleagues will give you a competitive edge. In addition, one of the secrets of being popular with customers and friends is to remember their names and the little things which make them feel they matter to you. This book explains clearly how you can maximise your memory in order to achieve your academic, professional and personal goals. Peter Marshall is a member of the Applied Psychology Research Group of the University of London and works primarily on research into superior memory. He recently assisted with the production of Channel 4's *Amazing Memory Show*. He is also author of *How To Study and Learn* in this series.

128pp. illus. 1 85703 234 9.

SELLING YOUR HOUSE
How to manage your agent, find the best buyer and complete the sale

Adam Walker

Almost everyone who has ever sold a house has a horror story to tell about the experience. This book explains in clear, jargon free terms, every stage of the sales process and gives an insider's view on how to avoid all the most common pitfalls. You will learn how to choose the right estate agent, how to set the optimum price for your property and negotiate an offer, and how to reduce the chances of a sale falling through. During his 15 years as a management consultant specialising in the residential property market, Adam Walker has advised more than 350 estate agency firms and trained more than 10,000 of their staff.

144pp. illus. 1 85703 287 X.

CONTROLLING ANXIETY
How to master fears and phobias and start living with confidence

William Stewart

Many people suffer from differing degrees of anxiety. Mild anxiety is a feeling common to us all – an unavoidable part of human personality. Severe anxiety on the other hand can control our lives. The aim of this book is to provide a knowledge base for sufferers and others, and to suggest strategies that will help people manage their anxiety and regain control of their lives. It is also a valuable handbook for those who work in healthcare and counselling. William Stewart is a freelance counsellor, supervisor and author. His background is in nursing, psychiatric social work, and student counselling and lecturing at a London college of nursing. He is author of *Self-Counselling* and co-author of *Learning to Counsel* in this series.

144pp. illus. 1 85703 267 5.

COPING WITH SELF ASSESSMENT
How to complete your tax return and minimise your tax bill

John Whiteley

Since its introduction in 1997, self assessment has become a fact of life for taxpayers. This book explains step by step how the system works, how to fill in your 1998/99 tax return, and how to avoid some of the pitfalls. There is also a chapter on how to pay less tax. Worked examples and illustrations are included throughout. John Whiteley FCA is a practising Chartered Accountant with long experience of advising taxpayers from every walk of life.

176pp. illus. 1 85703 470 8. 3rd edition.

ACHIEVING PERSONAL WELL-BEING
How to discover and balance your physical and emotional needs

James Chalmers

We tend to shut out natural daylight, work in soulless buildings, expose ourselves to pollution, and live on a diet of junk food. This highly original book is the result of a thorough investigation into how all these factors influence our physical and emotional welfare. It shows how daylight and the environment – including our astrological signs – determine our personality and health, and how by understanding their effects we can take steps towards achieving physical and emotional well-being. The author explores the interrelation of body and mind, and reveals how only by balancing and managing their combined needs can we achieve personal well-being in all aspects of our lives. James Chalmers BSc CEng MIEE is a scientist and an artist. In this book he combines reason and imagination to offer you a remedy for the pressures of modern living.

144pp. Illus. 1 85703 272 1.

MAKING A WEDDING SPEECH
How to prepare and deliver a memorable address

John Bowden

At thousands of weddings each year, many people are called on to 'say a few words'. But what do you say? How do you find the right words which will go down really well with the assembled company? Written by an experienced and qualified public speaker, this entertaining book shows you how to put together a simple but effective speech well suited to the particular occasion. Whether you are the best man, bridegroom, father of the bride or other participant, it will guide you every step from great opening lines to apt quotations, anecdotes, tips on using humour, and even contains 50 short model speeches you can use or adapt to any occasion.

176pp. 1 85703 385 X. 4th edition.

GUILDFORD **college**

Learning Resource Centre

Please return on or before the last date shown.
No further issues or renewals if any items are overdue.

2007 – 9 JAN 2011

0 8 NOV 2007 − 7 FEB 2012

2 5 MAR 2008 2 7 SEP 2012

– 3 JUN 2008
1 3 FEB 2009 – 7 OCT 2013

1 9 APR 2010 – 1 NOV 2018

– 7 JAN 2011

– 6 MAY 2011
1 4 JUN 2011

Class: 158.1 STE

Title: Building Self Esteem

Author: Stewart, William